Open My Heart, Heal My Soul

D1520423

Open My Heart, Heal My Soul

Living the Grace-Saturated Life

David P. Mann

RESOURCE *Publications* · Eugene, Oregon

OPEN MY HEART, HEAL MY SOUL
Living the Grace-Saturated Life

Resource Publications
An Imprint of Wipf and Stock Publishers
199 W. 8th Ave., Suite 3
Eugene, OR 97401

www.wipfandstock.com

ISBN 13: 978-1-62032-822-4

Manufactured in the U.S.A.

Contents

1

This Isn't Kansas Anymore

DO YOU EVER GET the sense that somehow something is missing in your life? Do you have the feeling that there should be more to your life than what you have experienced thus far . . . even as a Christian? Do you ever dwell on the poor choices that you've made (and possibly continue making) and beat yourself up over them thinking that you should be past these things by now in your walk with Christ? How about this one—do you feel like you've somehow left a part of you behind on the journey of life . . . and you miss you? If you answered "yes" to any of these questions, then read on.

When I was growing up, one of the movies that seemed to be an annual event on television was *The Wizard of Oz*. Dorothy and her little dog Toto were caught up in a twister that placed them in a strange new land called Oz. Here they wandered while seeking to find their way back home but it seemed at every turn that new and strange happenings occurred. Dorothy and Toto came upon three unusual individuals (the Tin Man, Cowardly Lion, and Scarecrow) along the way who all seemed to share something in common—they were focused on their personal deficits (heart, courage, and brain respectively) and desperately desired to be whole. They also shared with Dorothy a need to keep walking in search of finding what it was that they were missing.

Along the journey this cadre of travelers encountered obstacles and adversaries that sought to keep them from discovering what they so desperately desired. But they kept moving, together, for they believed that what they needed was just ahead . . . somewhere. They eventually came upon a little man whose ominous presence and reputation as the Wizard was but a series of illusions and trickery. Once the Wizard was shown to be who he really was (with the help of a pesky little terrier who didn't know any better than to tug on the curtain that kept the Wizard hidden from view and therefore larger than life), he wasn't nearly as intimidating. Eventually Dorothy, Toto, the Tin Man, Cowardly Lion, and the Scarecrow all received what they were pursuing—the return home to Kansas for Dorothy and Toto and the discovery of heart, courage, and brain for their friends. The movie ends with a bit of a twist in that it was all a dream—or was it?

The remarkable thing about some movies is how they can mirror life for us. I would say that this movie has a number of parallels with what I'd like to share in the pages that follow. To start with, it seems that many of us have some rather abrupt awakenings in life that match or surpass the twister that snatched up Dorothy's house and placed it, with a crash, in another land altogether. Not a land that was familiar or even desirable. In this strange land in which we find ourselves, we often seek desperately to find our way back home and encounter obstacles and adversaries along the way. Dissimilar to the movie, some of us find that we are not in a dream but rather a nightmare and that no matter how many times we repeat, "There's no place like home," we aren't afforded the opportunity to awaken in a safe and caring environment. We find out firsthand how painful it can be to live in a world that is far from what it should be yet having the hope that somehow it can be turned into something better.

We also meet fellow travelers along the way whom we walk with in a mutual pursuit of what we have lost or may never have felt that we possessed. The stories and needs may vary but the desire to be whole resonates with each one. We find comfort in the company of others on this journey and often try to pool our resources so as to help others find what it is that they are looking for. We suggest self-help books, counselors, seminars, retreats, healing ministries, and anything else that we have found helpful along the way. If we're fortunate enough, we find the supportive people, resources, and coping strategies to overcome what has stood in our way and even discover some wonderful new ways of viewing ourselves, God, our relationships, and our approach to life's challenges.

Another parallel between the movie and life has to do with the power of deception. The Wizard of Oz masterfully used pyrotechnics and other audio-visual means to intimidate others and to retain power in the land. Deception, as well as misperception, imprisons people in dungeons of distorted thinking and ways of behaving that when focused on to the exclusion of all else, keeps them from attaining all that God has created them to be. In other words, we may indeed be missing out on the rich blessing of living out our divine potential, or Grace-Saturated Narrative spoken of later on, to its fullest extent. Deception can be a thief of God's greatest plans for a person's life as we can become duped into thinking we must live far from the glory God intended for our lives because we're not good enough, spiritual enough, or some other "enough" that whispers in our ear. "If only you were more _____ ("together," "godly," etc.), then God might _____ ("love," "forgive," "embrace," etc.) you. But you're not!" Or even seemingly the opposite, "If only you were less _____ ("sinful," "carnal," "a mess," etc.), then God might _____ ("love," "forgive," "embrace," etc.) you. But you're not!" Deceptions totally negate the power of God and the rich grace that he offers us for our health and healing. Along with deception, we have an adversary who actively seeks to destroy us but will, if unable to do that, at least try to claim a partial victory by tricking us into living far below God's vast plans for our lives.

The View from Where I Stand

It's been said that where a person stands determines what they see. I've had opportunity to "stand" in different places on the journey of life that have allowed me to develop the perspectives that will be shared throughout this book. I've served in the roles of pastor, hospice chaplain, clinical counselor, and professor in a counselor education program. As a pastor I've met persons brand-new to the faith whose eyes were full of potential and pain. These folks had found faith in Christ and been wonderfully saved yet, like all of us, entered the family of God with "baggage" from life that needed to be "unpacked." Some of the baggage was painful and needing deep healing so as to experience all that God desired for their lives. I also found people who have served God for many years yet struggled to understand why, after so many years, they still had difficulty "putting off the old self and putting on the new self." After all, weren't all the "old self" practices supposed to drop off right away? Some of these people battled regularly with guilt when they looked at where they were and where they felt they *should have been by now* in their walk with God. The church also housed many people who were confident of their eternal destination yet were wondering what "abundant life" was all about. In other words, they were going to heaven but weren't really enjoying the trip.

For a time I served as a Hospice chaplain. Hospice is a wonderful organization that ministers to people who are in the final phase of dealing with terminal illness. Hospice seeks to help the patients and their families during this difficult time of life. In visiting with patients and their family members I gained a perspective of what is really important. It is amazing how dealing with one's own impending death or the death of a family member changes our outlook on life. It seems that whenever we are dealing with serious illness or death we give pause to what we've spent our life's energy in doing. For some, there is so much of life that has not been lived due to succumbing to the pressure from what someone once called "the tyranny of the urgent." All of us can be tempted to try to work through our "in boxes" of life tasks as if when we accomplished this feat, if attainable at all, *then* we'll spend more time with family and friends. But the "in box" is never empty when we die. Others look back and say that they wouldn't change a thing as they have lived their lives in such a way that they have little or no regrets. Near the end of our lives we also reflect on questions of meaning such as, "What was this all about?" and "What does it all mean?" We take stock of our lives and reflect on untapped potential and what *could have been.*

As a clinical counselor I have sat with countless people who have been wounded by others or by life in general. These people, dearly loved by God, had found that life truly is difficult and none of us receive a "get out of life free" card no matter how good or godly one is. Some of the people I've counseled with have awakened to find that their lives have somehow come into conflict with what they believed at one point, that they somehow have gotten off-track but never noticed it until they were way off-course. Like someone who was only two degrees off on their compass when they started out on the journey, but after walking this way for some time have found that they are a long way from where they believed they were heading. My clientele included pastors and missionaries, leaders and laity, individuals, couples, and entire families whose wounds needed care and counsel. Some became so focused on their problems, or the problems of those around them, that they had long lost sight of their position as sons and daughters of God and at times struggled to see themselves and others through the lens of God's grace. Others strove to become someone God never intended them to be so as to gain the acceptance of those around them only to find themselves endlessly pursuing "the me that *should be*" while hiding the me I really am.

As a professor of counseling I've had opportunity to help train some of the most gifted individuals who have answered the call of God to enter the ministry of professional counseling. As an integral part of this training paradigm we have focused on the *heart of the counselor* since that is where our own woundedness needs to be addressed before we're ever able to fully help those God brings our way in the counseling office. I like Henri Nouwen's term *Wounded Healer* as that is who we really are as we, along with our clients, pursue what God had in mind for us from the time he spoke us into existence. Not a problem-free life, but rather a grace-saturated approach to life wherein we live out fully *all* that God had in mind for us in this life.

Probably the best vantage point that I have is as a fellow journeyer in this life. Much of what I have discovered and will share in the pages that follow have been my own discoveries along the way. I, too, have found how difficult it is live out all that God had intended for my life while concurrently trying to "get life right" so as to "be right" with God, self and others. I can relate to whoever said, "It's awfully hard to concentrate on draining the swamp when you're up to your neck in alligators!" And so I tried harder to "get it right" in this life as if it was possible to reach a state of being where I was okay in the eyes of God and others with my efforts. "Perfectionism" robbed the joy from my life and also amplified the intensity of guilt that I felt for not having "my act together" while believing that *I should have by now*. Encountering God's rich grace frees me from the grasp of pursuing the idolatry of a perfect life and allows me to discover anew his great plans for my life—his grace-saturated life, or narrative, that he intended from the beginning that I live out. As a result, I am someone who sincerely believes that God is infinitely more grace-filled than we could ever imagine and has plans for our lives that are mind-boggling when we start to see them.

The Walking Wounded

The longer I live and the more I interact with others whose lives have been wounded, the more I realize that living can be hazardous to one's health. I'm just past the half century mark and as I reflect upon the collective events of my life and those of others I see a mixed bag that we carry. Some of the contents of this bag are things that have been priceless in their positive effect upon us, numerous happenings have been run of the mill "stuff" of life, and on the other end of the continuum are those challenging and often wounding experiences. All of the events combine to shape who we are today and yet many of us find it difficult to wrestle with our woundedness and therefore end up the "walking wounded" that we never would have imagined being.

What do the "walking wounded" look like? Exactly like you and me because we are they. In fact, I tell my counseling students that we are all "clients"—it's just some days we're in the counselor's seat in the counseling office. Some of us cover our wounds better than others and thereby avoid attention being drawn to our "limping" but we're all in this together. Does this mean that, as some would say, we're either in denial or recovery? Not at all. It does mean, however, that we live in a world that has been marred by sin's impact and is not functioning as it was created to. We, as part of that creation, are also impacted by sin in that we are not as safe with one another and our world as we were designed to be. We have been wounded by sin, and we have the choice every day where we will place our life choices on the continuum of unhealthy to healthy principles and practices (i.e., to be agents of healing or further wounding). It is not by mistake that part of the Lord's Prayer is that we ask for his kingdom to come and his will be done on earth as it is in heaven. Why? Because when God's kingdom principles and practices are truly being lived out, we heal from our wounds and the thoughts, feelings, and behaviors that result from them, and have the opportunity to develop healing communities that invite others to enter in.

What's Ahead

As with any journey it is best to take a look at the map before departing. In the pages ahead I'll spend some time laying the foundation by taking a look at where we find ourselves in this world that we live in (Chapter 2). We'll gain a worldview that helps us make sense of the events taking place all around us and their impact upon us. I'll then talk about our hearts as the center of who we are and how being wounded in life affects us at the deepest level of our being (Chapter 3). When wounded we tend to cover up and protect ourselves which keeps us from really living the life that God intended for us to live. I'll then present a new way of looking at the problems that develop in our lives as a result of our woundedness that will enable the reader to approach problems in a much different way (Chapter 4). Our attention will then turn toward gaining an understanding of God's thick and rich grace and the powerful role it plays as we journey through life (Chapter 5). Once we gain a better understanding of grace for ourselves and others, we are better positioned to become people whose very presence emanates the Grace of God to others (Chapter 6). Embracing grace gives us a new perspective on the struggles we and others have and empowers us to live out courageously the kind of life that God has designed for us (Chapter 7).

2

Where Are We?

NOT LONG AGO THERE was a commercial on television that showed a couple driving along in their new truck. As they were traveling, the wife is asking her husband how he likes each of the various features of the new vehicle and receives back from him answers that show that he really likes them. She then asks the question that was brewing underneath for some time—how did he like the built-in navigational system? When he responded that he also liked it she said, "Then why don't you use it?" It is at this point that the camera takes us outside of the vehicle to see that this new truck they are traveling in is on a road in the desert . . . but hauling a boat! The husband then says, "This is starting to look familiar" as he turns off the highway. The reason this commercial was able to make its point was because we can all relate to being lost while at the same time thinking that if we just keep traveling, we'll figure out where we are.

As we begin this journey of healing we need to "check our navigational system" for a few minutes to gain an understanding of where we are and where we would like to be so that we can plan out how we will arrive at our desired destination. What we need is an understanding of the world around and within us so we can travel with wisdom. Without such an understanding, we may continue to travel along having no idea where we're going . . . but feeling like we're making really good time!

The View from Above

For us to really know where we are so that we can plan where we would like to go, we need to gain a view from above. By this I mean we need to gain a much bigger perspective than many of us have as we are dealing with life on a daily basis. We need first to have an understanding that God created and loves each of us and has a wonderful story (or narrative) that he desires each of us to live out in our lifetimes. The impact of sin upon this world and all that God has created, however, is immense and its impact upon human beings precipitated our separation from God. Christ came that he might save, heal and deliver us from the bondage of sin. When we respond to his invitation through the Spirit's calling, we enter right relationship with him. It is at this point that our lives are made new and we *have the opportunity* to live out God's divine potential and plan for our lives. When we live in this way the kingdom of God truly does come to earth and God's will truly is done on earth as it is in heaven. We have an adversary, however, named Satan who actively works contrary to God's plans and seeks to thwart these plans by a variety of means of deception and dirty tricks.

The starting point for us is to see that we are spiritual and physical beings living in a battle zone where God and Satan both have plans for us as individuals, families, and the larger communities in which we live—that couldn't be more polar opposite! This is clearly seen in a foundational passage of Scripture from the Gospel of John: "The thief comes only to steal and kill and destroy; I have come that they may have life, and have it to the full." (10:10, NIV). From this we see that the thief, Satan, is intent on doing as much damage and destruction as he possibly can to all that God has created—which includes you and me. The verse points out that Satan "comes only" to do these wicked things which is borne out also in the words of another translation, "The thief's *purpose* is to steal and kill and destroy" (NLT; emphasis added). It is Satan's purpose and plan to oppose God and all that God has created and values in every conceivable way possible. Why? Because he and all of his forces are at war with God and all those loyal to him. Both are seeking to impact this world but God has a plan for our good: "My purpose is to give life in all its fullness" (NLT). I also like how the Amplified Version portrays this verse: "The thief comes only in order to steal and kill and destroy. I came that they may have *and* enjoy life, and have it in abundance (to the full, till it overflows)."

The first 18 verses of John 10 are an amazing account of Jesus trying to convey to the people what is going on in this world and the reason for him coming to live and die the sacrificial life that he did. He tried to point out to them that they were in peril of being harmed by thieves and robbers posing as their shepherd while all along they really only had one true Shepherd who cared for them with an intense love and commitment. By the time we come to verse 10 we find him pointing out the intentions of the thieves and robbers as compared to the wonderful plan he has for his sheep. As we begin this journey, we need to keep in the very forefront of our minds that we have a wonderful Shepherd, Jesus, who sees our condition here on earth and cared enough to do something about it. Something that caused him great agony and death but resulted in his victory over the very thing that has infected the world that he made—sin. He conquered sin and its subsequent effect, eternal separation from our Creator, and made a way for us to enjoy the life he created us to have. And that wasn't all of it. He also made it possible for us to experience life beyond mere existence; he made it possible to have life *to the full* as compared to what a friend of mine calls "benign existence." Our Shepherd is still active in our world through the work of the Holy Spirit who lives within us and seeks to have us cooperate with his plans for our lives and the world around us. How does he do this? By teaching us his ways through the Scriptures and through his invitations to healthy living. He not only desires that we live in a way that pleases him and brings health to this world, he empowers us to live in such a way. It still is our choice, however, whether we will cooperate with the Spirit or not in our life decisions. We are choosing beings and will make many, many choices each day that have significance for our lives and others. Satan is also aware of this fact and desires to have us cooperate with his plans instead. I'll write more on Satan's impact on our choices later in this chapter.

So to begin, we need to understand that the world we live in has a number of active players in it—and not all have the intention of God's ways being lived out here on earth. As noted above, God is actively at work in the world he has created. God is a God who still communicates with us, albeit not usually in ways like we communicate with each other. I like how Philip Yancey phrased God's way of communicating with humans as "correspondence." God indeed does correspond with us through his word being brought to life as we read and reflect on it, through others whose grace-filled lives give evidence of God's indwelling Spirit, through intuitive means wherein we may "hear" him speak a word to us in our thoughts, and in a variety of other ways all congruent with the principles of Scripture. More on *correspondence* in chapter 7.

Satan and all of his forces are actively at work tempting and deceiving human beings in any way that he/they can. I unapologetically believe in such an evil being as shown in Scripture and although I wish he could be seen as wearing a red suit while carrying a pitchfork, that so under-describes this powerful, created being that it sets us up to underestimate his ways by relegating him to some sort of Halloween character. He is very active at seeking to destroy God's creation as noted earlier and so I refer to him often in the paragraphs that follow. Lest one think that this seminary professor has gone loony in such a day of reason, others may choose to describe the power of sin incarnate in the world in different ways which is fine with me. I choose to utilize the name used in Scripture in the discussion that follows.

Another player, actually a whole host of them, is active in this world as well. You and I and the millions of other human beings play a role in what happens every day here on earth. We cannot simply say, as the comedian Flip Wilson of years gone by stated in his routine, "The devil made me do it!" No, the devil may be working desperately to seek to have us cooperate with his plans through evil actions or our part, but he does not *make* us do these things—he *invites* us to and we are free to choose not to. This, by the way, is true also of the leading of God's Spirit in our lives. He will not *make* us live in conformity with God's ways but he will *invite* us to cooperate with his plans that will bring about more of what he desires in and through our lives. (See Galatians Chapter 5 for further discussion of cooperating, or walking, with the Spirit or in the flesh [i.e., cooperating with temptations afforded by Satan to humanity's proclivities toward sin]).

One other "player" on the field of our lives and that being the randomness of timing and nature. Each of us holds to varied views of how much "chance" happens in this world so I won't take time to detail them. I'd prefer we see that on a continuum between total freedom and determinism we all choose a spot to stand with our beliefs. For a number of things in life, there is a certain amount of chance involved. For example, the likelihood that I will get the parking spot closest to my destination is a matter of chance and timing, with peak business hours increasing the chances against it. Being in the right or wrong place at the right or wrong time also has an element of chance involved yet God can and does at times orchestrate that we be where he desires us to be exactly when he desires us to be there.

Nature has a certain amount of freedom too as I see it. Some of the acts of nature can be traumatic but even these tend to be cause and effect happenings that occur in a world where God has set into motion some rules governing the planet. For example, too much rain coinciding with not enough ground cover acting in accordance with laws of gravity on the sides of steep banks create conditions in which mudslides can happen. I'd like to think that God is especially pleased with me by sending sunshine and warm weather on a day where I have a free enough schedule to ride my motorcycle but the truth is, the "rain falls on the just and unjust" and so, in Ohio anyway, the sunny day might be just a random happening.

Why do I spend time laying such a foundation? It is important for us to see that on any given day, the world that we experience is a combination of forces at work. Although I will spend a majority of time on the work of Satan, the enemy of our souls, and how he gets humans to cooperate with his plans to bring about the wounding of hearts and souls, I will also talk about the healing power of God at work in our world and how our Lord also invites us to cooperate with these plans for the world in which we live.

Imago Dei Under Attack

We are made in the image of God (Imago Dei) and I suspect that in itself makes us objects of wrath in Satan's eyes. But what exactly does it mean to be made in God's image? In short, we are thinking, feeling, acting, relational beings that have great capacity for impacting the world around us. When we follow God's plans for how we conduct ourselves on this planet that he has created, life is really good for all of God's creation. Satan must have had a suspicion of this when he deceived the first human beings to make some decisions that had short-term enjoyment with long-lasting devastation. It doesn't take one long to read in the creation story how the act of violating God's guidelines for living (i.e., don't eat of *that* tree) opened the eyes of their understanding to issues that we continue to grapple with today. Just a couple bear mentioning. First, Adam and Eve's act of disobedience to "garden rules" impacted their relationship with God. For the first time ever, they were no longer able to walk with him as was their standard daily activity but were now removed from the garden altogether. In that very same instance, they became more than aware of their nakedness. They also became acutely aware of the emotion we call shame. So they began covering up in order to avoid such feelings. Do you and I continue to deal with such things as feeling distant from God and struggling with shame? Indeed many of us do, and this is all connected to a decision that was made centuries ago by our first parents—at the prompting of the serpent.

But God created us, loves us, and values us to the point that redemption's plan involved the offering of Jesus' life as a sacrifice to reclaim us. God also has created us all with the variety we find in the millions of different people with whom we share this planet. Every one of us being unique in who we are and what we are like. In fact, as I teach a class on human growth and development, I am always amazed at the likelihood of any one of us becoming who we are when we consider the odds of that happening from the combination of our parents' DNA. Will we have our father's eyes, nose, eye color, disposition, proclivities toward health or disease or our mother's height, facial features, smile, and similar personality? It's all there for the combination into who we are today but the odds of you being exactly like you are is astronomical! And I've only noted the things that our parents contribute to the person we are—what about God's plans for who we, as integrated individuals in interaction with others, are to be and become? That adds in another dimension altogether that we might see as the "reason" for us being who we were created to be. From a Christian worldview we might use the term *teleology* to describe the purpose for our existence here on earth as opposed to simply seeing ourselves from a naturalistic viewpoint. Why are we as we are and to what end are we created? That is something that speaks of life beyond simply living and to which I will return in later chapters when I write about our Grace Saturated Narratives.

The Enemy of Our Souls

Back to John 10:10 as this is a foundational passage of Scripture for us to consider. Since Satan is opposed to all that God values, he wants to "steal, kill, and destroy" anything that he can. Is it any wonder that he is referred to as the enemy of our souls? Scripture is filled with references to him and his work and guess what? He is not finished yet. He is all about destruction, deceit, and anything else that flies in the face of God and what he desires.

What exactly does Satan seek to steal, kill, and destroy? Anything he can! His goal is to annihilate anything he can but since this is not possible (due to God standing in the way), he seems to settle for lesser wins. Let me explain. If Satan could get us to utterly destroy each other, he most certainly would give that his best effort. Since, however, God will not allow him to have such widespread destruction, he will settle for getting human beings to turn on each other for a wide variety of reasons—reasons that all seem to make sense to us at the time or we wouldn't do them. We do see such mass destruction of lives at the hands of fellow human beings. Why? Because our world (inside and out) is not the way God originally created it *and* we have an active adversary trying to work this to his advantage.

But let me share just a few examples that Satan goes after in our everyday lives. First, he attacks our choices. Every day when we awake we are met with a day full of choices to be made. Some of these choices are as benign as what kind of cereal we would like for breakfast. Other choices have more weight to them as to which kingdom values and principles (God's or Satan's) are put into play in this world; in your world and mine. Take for example what we think about, what we speak about, how we spend our time and money. These are all choices that can have a profound effect upon the world around us—for good or evil. As I have been watching the news of late, one particular news program has been highlighting people who are making a positive difference in these difficult times. Those highlighted are ordinary folks like you and me who have decided to do something good for others without expecting anything in return. Decisions such as these lead to actions that make this world a better place for us to live in together. Are these people all professing to be followers of Christ? I have no idea. What I do know is that their decisions are in line with what God is looking for in our decisions for this world. On the other hand, we've all seen and heard accounts on the news that leave us wondering how people could be so evil in their decisions when we hear of those taking advantage of the elderly, or harming children and others. Of what kingdom are their choices in alignment? It seems obvious.

But are choices a simple matter? I don't think so. We need to have a better understanding of how choices are made, the process behind them so that we do a better job with our choices. In other words, if we have no idea how we got to the point of making particular choices, how will we know how to overcome bad ones in the future? More on choices in the chapters that follow.

Another area of attack is how we look at life. In other words, Satan seeks to steal our ability to see the world around us appropriately. Interpretations of life's events are what we get when we view life through our particular set of "lenses." Although much of how we come to develop our particular lenses in life have to do with events and things we have experienced and learned growing up (spoken of later in the next chapter), Satan seeks to influence the way we look at life by influencing the choices and events involving others so that we are more prone to develop distorted lenses. Distorted lenses cause us to see life very differently. In a very simple example, I wear eyeglasses and if I didn't clean them, I would likely complain about how dirty everything looked around me. Is the world dirtier than usual? No, but the lenses I am looking through, if I am unaware that they are covered with dust and dirt, will give a different view than others would see.

Satan is also spoken of as a liar and the father of lies (John 8:44). But what exactly is a lie? A lie is something that is false being made out to be true. So when we read that Satan is the father of lies and lying is his native tongue, know that he seeks to get us to believe his lies about all areas of our lives and therefore distort negatively our views of self, God, others, and life itself. And he is good at it too! Remember when Jesus was being tempted in the desert place? Satan even quoted Scripture as a means of trying to tempt Jesus. But Jesus called him on this and showed that Satan was actually misquoting Scripture to use it in an evil way. In effect, he was lying through massaging the words found in Scripture to make them say what *he* intended them to say and passing them off as what the Scriptures were saying. This is an especially insidious approach wherein Satan knows that if he can distort the Truth to the point of being a keenly disguised lie, it is even more powerful to those who value Scripture as a guide for living.

A Moment for Reflection. Some reading this book need to sit with that last paragraph for a bit and ask some questions of themselves. It is a very common experience among Christian folks to believe a misquoted Scripture passage to the point where it is personally detrimental. So my question to you is this: Is there a particular passage of Scripture that seems to point a finger of condemnation at you? Your spouse? Your children? Your God? Or anyone else in your life? If so, I'd encourage you to do some research on the passage of Scripture to see if you really understand it in context. A number of commentaries and Bible helps are available. You might check with your pastor or other respected Christian leader as well as at the Christian bookstore for such resources. Satan would love you to misquote Scripture so that it steals joy and relationships from you. Satan's lies and distortions are manipulations of our minds for the sake of harming us. And, as I have noted above, he is good at what he does.

Have you ever watched a professional magician and been totally confounded by what they did? In fact, possibly the illusion that they performed was so good that it made your head hurt trying to figure it out—without success of course! These individuals, if they are to make a living at this, must hone their skills to the point where what they do actually does distort the reality of the audience. People are all different, however, and so not all audiences need such sophistication to be misled. I recall one day being with a friend who was a real clown—the kind with make-up, balloons, and magic tricks. He was entertaining a small child by making a beanbag disappear right before the child's eyes. The child laughed with glee each time and kept asking him to do it again. As I watched, my friend was simply distracting the child and flipping the beanbag over the child's head to land behind them without the child being aware of it. Then he would open his hand to show that indeed the beanbag had disappeared. I thought about how easily it was to trick someone who couldn't see what I saw. Now imagine, if you will, a being that does not die and is bent on evil. Over the centuries, this evil being has watched people and seen how they are best misled and has developed a series of "tricks" that he tries out on them with great success. You're getting the picture about our adversary. Satan would not be successful at what he does if he were not really good at deception. Deception is only good when it works.

Think about it for a second. If we really saw the results of giving into temptation *beforehand*, is there as much a chance that we would do so? Maybe not. If we could *see* what was beyond the temptation we hopefully would run away more often but we don't because we can be deceived into thinking what is wrong is right and what is right is wrong. We, like the child I mentioned above, can gleefully be distracted away from what is really happening while being enamored by the "magic trick" before our eyes.

Another of Satan's favorite ploys is when he seeks to trick us into thinking that we *are* the problem rather than dealing *with* the problems of our lives. Although I'll write more about this in a later chapter, let me say that this is an area of great struggle for many Christians. We all make mistakes, we all sin, we all struggle in many ways as we are learning to put off our old ways of living. Satan knows that some of us believe we ought to be able to do this by ourselves and fail miserably at times. He also knows that shame and condemnation are powerful emotional issues to deal with and so he heaps heavy doses of both upon us whenever we do sin. Along with shame and condemnation, he also tries to tell us that we not only *shouldn't* (by the way, shoulds and shouldn'ts induce guilt and shame) have done what we said or did, but also that we *shouldn't be the way we are*. See how easily and craftily he makes us *into* the problems that we struggle with? More to say on this later.

Relationships are another realm that is under attack and this, too, is a strategic area to target. As noted earlier, in being made in the likeness of

God we are created to be relational people. It makes sense then that Satan would apply his tricks and tactics in his assault on our relationships. In his watching of humanity over time he has seen the wonderful things people can accomplish together when working in harmony. He has also seen what great devastation can occur when people turn on one another. If he can, with his tricks and schemes, get people to turn on one another he can wreak great havoc against God's intended plans for humanity.

One of the ways our relationships are under attack is through misunderstandings that are viewed as "facts." Over the years I have counseled a number of couples and families for a variety of issues. One that seems to crop up enough that it has become a commonality in everyday talk is "communication problems." I have often re-titled this common problem as no longer a communication problem but rather an "understanding" problem. Semantics? I don't believe so. Here's why. If it was simply a communication problem, we could work primarily on words chosen, nonverbal communication skills, listening skills, etc. to solve the problem. Although this may be included in the process of counseling for "understanding" problems, it may not be the totality of it. However, a problem of understanding goes deeper still. If a person does not feel "heard" to the level of being understood and valued, we will only be addressing surface issues and debating whether what was said is true or false. Often I'll hear, "That's not what I meant" only to be answered with "But that's what you said!" Misunderstandings can eventually lead to solidified beliefs about those we are in relationship with and Satan knows this. It is as if when we are mulling over painful words that have been spoken that we can almost hear a whisper in our heart's ear that says, "You know that's what she meant" about some negative interpretation we are nursing. Relational lies in the making.

Another way that relationships come under attack is through the process of objectification. When we turn people into objects, we can do all sorts of evil against them or use them as objects for our own gratification. I recall watching a television show where a person who had been incarcerated for targeting tourists and breaking into their cars to steal all they had was being interviewed. The person had since done their time in prison and was now helping law enforcement officials in trying to stop such crimes. The interviewer asked the poignant question, "Did you ever stop to consider that these were families on vacation that you were stealing from and ruining their time together?" to be met quickly with, "I couldn't think of them that way or I could have never done it." No longer families, simply objects that could part with their possessions. In working with men who struggle with pornography, objectification of women is one of the issues that we address. As long as these images are of nameless women, they remain objects to be used for sexual gratification. However, when one begins to see these women as someone's sister, daughter, or mother, it can begin to challenge one's thinking about them.

Even our mental and emotional health isn't safe from the enemy's attacks. Our emotions and thought life are so powerful and so interconnected that it makes sense that this would be a target area. When our minds are clear, it's amazing how much we can accomplish and create. When our emotions are well, we can garner the energy to live life with vitality, fully engaged in the things we are committed to. When our thoughts and emotions become difficult to bear, we have a hard time experiencing the life God gives us, much less the abundant kind he offers. I've counseled numbers of people dealing with forms of anxiety, depression, guilt and despair connected to living with the memories of failures and wounds. The enemy would love to keep us in such a place of pain for we are not only tormented with life, we're in a state of what I call "emotional nausea" where we seemingly cannot muster the energy to live our lives for fear of feeling worse. Like a broken record, we keep spinning round and round in our minds the things we have done (personal failures and the wounds they have caused others) or have been done to us by the actions and words of others. If the enemy can keep us hurting in the depths of our hearts and souls, he can keep us from living life to the full in the way God intended for us to live.

Satan has even stolen people's stories, or narratives, that God planned for them to live out. He is intent on doing anything possible to destroy us—including stealing our potential God has created within each of us. I heard a saying that goes along this line, "Satan takes us farther than we want to go, charges us more than we want to pay, and keeps us longer than we'd like to stay." How does he do this? Generally a little at a time. When this occurs over time, we not only lose out on the things that we have been "over-charged" for by Satan, we tend to believe certain lies as well. We tend to lose our belief in ourselves and find distance between the person we once believed ourselves to be and the person we see in the mirror each day.

God created each of us with unique giftings, talents, personalities, and plans for how these could be fully lived out in this life to the glory of God and the enhancement of our world. I have referred to this as our Grace-Saturated Narrative in a later chapter but need to point out here that

Satan is *very interested* in attacking this area of our lives. Why? Simple. Our Grace-Saturated Narrative is comparable to a divine version of our life DNA. God has created each of us different than anyone else because he delights in variety and his creativity cannot be constrained. He is our Creator and if he is fully able to make every snowflake different and fill the skies with more stars than can ever be counted, how could he constrain himself to using a cookie-cutter approach to humanity? Again, Satan knows this and hates anything God delights in. If God truly delights in creating us all different and not only redeems us from our sins but also desires to have us live life abundantly, I cannot help but think he has unique plans for each of us. When we discover and live out these plans so that our lives resemble as closely as possible all that he designed them to be, one can only imagine the impact upon the world in which we live!

When our Grace-Saturated Narratives are stolen or muddied beyond visibility, it leaves us experiencing less than the abundant life due to living below the potential for which we were created. Sometimes these stories are lost in replacement stories that the enemy of our souls dupes us into embracing as our own. Sometimes, just as he used distorted Scripture to tempt Jesus in the wilderness, he can use other distortions of stories tied to our faith to tempt us into becoming something we are not in an attempt to feel acceptance for who we are. When you've been duped into thinking, for example, that you have to be perfect based on the passage of Scripture that says, "Be ye therefore perfect, even as your Father which is in heaven is perfect" (Matthew 5:48), you are boxed in *if* you don't understand what the verse is saying. It is *not* saying that you must reach perfection as in flawlessness since the original word for perfection, as used here, is described in the following way according to Barclay's *The Gospel of Matthew*:

> The Greek word for *perfect* is *teleios*. The word often is used in Greek in a very special way. It has nothing to do with what we might call abstract, philosophical, metaphysical perfection . . . A man who has reached his full-grown stature is *teleios* in contradistinction to a half-grown lad . . . To put it another way, the Greek idea for perfection is *functional*. A thing is perfect if it fully realizes the purpose for which it was planned, and designed, and made. In point of fact, that meaning is involved in the derivation of the word. *Teleios* is an adjective formed from the noun *telos*. *Telos* means an end, a purpose, an aim, a goal. A thing is *teleios*, if it realizes the purpose for which it was planned; a man is perfect if he realizes the purpose for which he was created and sent into the

world. So then, a man will be *teleios* if he fulfills the purpose for
which he was created. (*Volume 1*, pp. 177-178)

Did you see that? If we believe the lie that we must become faultless,
without error, sinless, we will forever be chasing a fantasy of who we think
we *should be* rather than seeking to attain who God has created us to be
(Grace-Saturated Narrative). We will of necessity try to fit into another
"skin" than our own seeking to meet all "conditions of acceptance" set out
by others. Often these conditions are fostered by others whom we respect
but who also have misinterpreted this passage of Scripture. Such misunderstood Scriptures invite us to be different than we really are, different than
who God desires us to be.

> *A Moment for Reflection.* For all of us recovering or active perfectionists,
> this is really good news not to be passed over lightly. Sit with it for a bit
> and ask yourself, "What would my life be like if I truly believed that God
> wasn't looking for perfection in how I live but rather desired that I discover
> who I was created to be . . . and live in that 'skin' without apology?"

Unmasking the Enemy

There is good news in all of this talk on Satan and his dealings. We are *not
ignorant of what he is up to* according to 2 Corinthians 2:11. "And what
I have forgiven—if there was anything to forgive—I have forgiven in the
sight of Christ for your sake, in order that Satan might not outwit us. *For we
are not ignorant of his schemes*" (NIV, emphasis added). The word ignorant
has often been used in a pejorative way by people (e.g., "You're just being
ignorant!") to the point that we can miss its real meaning. It actually refers
to us lacking knowledge or comprehension of a thing such as, in this case,
what the enemy is up to. Once we pick up on it though, we are in a much
better position to overcome such schemes and devices that he uses.

In the opening chapter I referred to the little terrier Toto in the
movie *The Wizard of Oz* and how he pulled back the curtain to reveal
the source of the loud, booming voice of the Wizard. Here stood a man
using various forms of audio-visual means to make himself bigger than
life. Similar to the movie, Satan knows he is no match for the risen son
of God and the Spirit he has sent to live in us. I also think that Satan will

keep using his same bag of tricks until *we* discover what he is up to and take appropriate steps to avoid his traps.

Scripture goes on to tell us, "We demolish arguments and every pretension that sets itself up against the knowledge of God, and we take captive every thought to make it obedient to Christ" (2 Corinthians 10:5). This speaks also to our part in the process. We not only learn to identify what Satan is up to, we also learn to discern truth from error so that we do not continue to believe the lies we have believed from Satan or others in our lives that detract from or steal our Grace-Saturated Narratives.

Wounded in this Battle Zone

As I have discussed in this chapter, we are in a battle zone where Satan and his allies are seeking to destroy anything and anyone of value to God. He has a variety of ways of attempting this and one of the main means of accomplishing his goals is to get us to cooperate with him. Many of us have felt the pain of being wounded by others in this life. These woundings have gone deeper than our flesh to wound us at our very core. We have experienced the wounding of our hearts and souls.

3

Hearts and Souls Under Attack

THE STORY IS TOLD that one winter morning, before heading off to school, a young boy left his house to do one of his assigned chores—take the garbage out. But this morning would prove to be different than any other morning as a series of events unfolded that affected his life for years to come. It seems that not only was he aware of his weekly duty of taking the trash cans to the curb, so were some of the neighborhood kids who, on this morning, lay in wait to ambush him with snowballs.

Surprise Attack

As the boy placed the last can next to the road he was struck in the head by the first snowball, knocking his stocking cap clean off. Dazed, he looked around to see what was happening only to be pelted with more that hit him in the chest, leg, and shoulder in successive thuds. Almost without thinking, he grabbed one of the lids off of a trash can and wielded it like a shield to protect himself from the onslaught of frozen projectiles as he worked his way back to the safety of his house. He found the "shield" he had chosen worked very well as he blocked snowball after snowball with it until he was safely inside. Winded and worried now about walking to school, he came up with a plan—he would carry the trash can lid with him to school *just in case he needed it again!*

The boy snatched up his book bag and just before opening the door, took a firm grip on his new "shield," cautiously leaving the house. He moved slowly down the sidewalk looking first this way then that to see if anyone who had previously attacked him was there. "Nope, no one" he thought as he continued down the walkway. "I wonder if they are up ahead?" he thought, as he tightened his grip on the "shield." Block after block he was both relieved that no more snowballs were being thrown and anxious that it could be just around the next corner that he would meet with another attack.

Hiding Our Shields

Once arriving at school, he breathed a sigh of relief as he entered the heavy doors of the building. As he took his jacket off and unpacked his books from the bag, he realized that he had to do something with the lid—but what? After all, it protected him so well from an earlier attack, maybe it could spare him from other "attacks" that may come that day. So he took it to class with him and set it neatly beside his desk, as best as possible out of the sight of others.

Day after day, week after week the boy carried the garbage can lid with him everywhere he went and felt the security of it even though it kept him from using both hands for the activities of the day. After a while his friends began questioning why he carried the "shield" and he often concocted various stories to try to avoid attention—but with little success. Years went by and people began to keep their distance from him since the "shield" was not very inviting to be near. The boy had become a young man now and began to have questions about himself that included, "What's wrong with me that I can't seem to get near to people without fear?" and "Why do I find it so hard to let go of the 'shield' when it has far outlived its usefulness?" He felt stuck and wished he could be free—but how?

I don't recall where I first came upon a similar version of this story but it so resonated with what I have seen in people's lives that I have retold it a number of times over the years. You see, the little boy represents many of us who had been going about our own business when suddenly we were met with a flurry of attacks. These attacks weren't snowballs, however, but they scared and wounded us to the point that we desperately sought ways of protecting ourselves from further wounds. To our relief, the various "shields" that we picked up and wielded did indeed protect us *then*. But after years of carrying these shields, we have become weary of the toll that has been exacted as a result. What at first became a shield for our wounded hearts and souls has now become a way of life that imprisons and weighs heavily upon us.

Walls That Protect and Imprison

There is such a wide variety of ways that people have been wounded in childhood, adolescence, and adulthood that it would take entire books to name them all if that was possible to do. What we do have in common, however, is that these things can affect us to the point that we build walls around our hearts in an attempt to protect ourselves from other hurts. These walls begin by protecting us but in the end imprison as we build the walls higher and higher. Walls effectively close off our hearts from such pain again . . . but at what price? Overly shielded hearts become closed hearts that have a hard time letting others, including God, inside for fear of further pain. So we walk through life heavily shielded yet desiring to let down the walls to be fully ourselves again or, if we cannot remember a time without a shield, to be our true selves for the first time.

Heart and Soul

To begin this journey of opening our hearts and finding healing for our souls we must first begin with an understanding of what we're talking about. Often when people speak of their hearts they are referring to that feeling, sensing, trusting center of their being. That is partially true but it is much more than that. It is also the place where we hold people, places, and memories dear to us along with where we experience brokenness, wounds, regrets, and fear. When people speak of their souls, however, they describe that part of their being that embraces the Divine. In some circles, the soul is what is saved for eternity from what otherwise would be a state of eternal damnation. It is that "spiritual" aspect of us that has eternal value. While these opening definitions carry some measure of truth to how heart and soul may differ, the terms are more similar than dissimilar.

The Center of Our Being

From the beginning God created us as integrated persons whose hearts and souls combined to make up the persons we were created to be. The heart is that center of our being where all the thoughts, intentions, commitments, choices, and feelings reside. Some would even equate the mind and heart as they seem to be used somewhat interchangeably throughout Scripture.

When we commit our lives to Christ we may refer to this as asking Jesus "into our hearts" to become our Lord and Savior. But what does that mean? It refers to a surrender of my life to God by accepting the forgiveness offered through the sacrificial life, death, and resurrection of Jesus Christ. Where does this take place? In the very core of my being, my "heart" so to speak for it is there that I daily choose to follow him and his ways.

It is also in the heart that we experience the peace of God that comes as a result of inviting the Savior to forgive all my sin and free me from its power. So what, then, is "saved"? My "soul" which includes all of me. In fact, the word has often been used when describing people who have lost their lives (e.g., "Three souls were lost at sea when the boat capsized."). So when I speak of "opening" our hearts and experiencing healing for our "souls" I am referring to the fact that many of us have experienced such woundings in our lives that we have found ways of closing off our hearts from experiencing any more pain. We may or may not realize that the wounds we experience are not simply memories that we hold in our hearts, they have permeated our total being to the point that *all* of our being, our *soul*, needs to find healing at the deepest levels—to the depth of our souls. Yet to get at such levels of personhood, we must first go through the door of the heart.

Pay Attention to Your Heart

In the Book of Proverbs we find some profound information about the center of our beings, our hearts. "Above all else" the Scripture says, "guard your heart for it is the wellspring of life" (4:23). "Above all else" in life seems to indicate how important it is that we guard our hearts. But why? The rest of the verse explains that the heart is the "wellspring of life." This captures my imagination. "Wellspring" can be defined as "an original and bountiful source of something" (Oxford American Dictionaries) and "a source of continual supply" (Merriam-Webster Online). No wonder the guarding of the heart is so important for if it can be polluted or damaged in some way, our source of life now has been compromised.

Imagine that someone had a "wellspring" of water that they continually drew from each day for themselves, their family members, and their livestock. They also drew from this source to water their gardens to provide food for their family. But one night some enemy sneaked in and polluted the wellspring. When the person now tasted the water they knew something was terribly wrong and so they sought ways of correcting the problem but didn't guard it. The next night the same enemy now sneaked in and damaged the wellspring so that no one could draw water from it. This would be a tremendous loss and the result of not having built some type of protective fence around their source of life.

Imagine further that the owner of the wellspring became so fearful of another attack by their enemy that they did more than correct the problem of the contaminated water—they built an impenetrable wall around the wellspring that not only kept the enemy from attacking again, it also kept the family from being able to access the water. That picture helps us see how important it is to protect our hearts while being careful not to allow these attacks to tempt us into so protecting ourselves so well that we are unable to access the life that it contains. This would be the case of the young man with the garbage can lid as a defense noted earlier.

Where Thoughts Become Actions

There are many other passages of Scripture that speak of the heart but I want to draw attention to one more that is found in the Book of Matthew. "For out of the overflow of the heart the mouth speaks" (Matthew 12:34). There is a key principle here that often gets overlooked. This passage draws a clear connection between what is in our hearts and what becomes action. So, for example, if we reflect upon positive events in our hearts, we likely will have these very same positive thoughts become words which is why other passages of Scripture encourage us to think on "whatsoever things are good."

This very principle is also shown in what Jesus shared in Chapter 5 as well when speaking of lust and anger that are not dealt with in the heart. In verses 27-28 Jesus points out that not only is it wrong to actually commit adultery, one who looks lustfully at others has committed adultery already in their hearts. We have to see the principle that both Matthew 5 and 12 are conveying to us—that it really does matter what we hold in our hearts. He is showing us that those things that get into our hearts and poison the "wellspring," if not dealt with, will eventually develop into even bigger things when they "go live" into our words and actions.

> *A Moment for Reflection.* In my experience as a counselor and pastor I've come across people who misunderstand what is being conveyed in Matthew 5. When I've been told, "Well, thinking it is as bad as doing it" I know they have a fundamental error that, left unaddressed, can lead to some bad outcomes. One of the bad outcomes is we can say, "Well, since I've already sinned in my thoughts, I might as well do it!" This places the person at risk of acting out in ways that can be very destructive. Another bad outcome is to feel *as if* I've already done something bad because I thought about it. This places a person into the position where they often feel guilty for things they never have done but, because they equate "thinking it" with "doing it," somehow elicit the same guilt and shame as might come had they *actually done it* (whatever "it" might be). Our thought life is the spiritual battlefield where we wrestle to decide what we will do. The principle here is that we need to deal with the thought life so as to have it turn into a good action.

Using the example Jesus gave of lust in the heart and adultery, we need to see these as points on a continuum. On the one end we would have the initial sighting of a person who is attractive to us and on the other end is the inappropriate acting out of sexual desire with them. The principle involved here is that we must deal with it in the early stages of thought rather than allow the initial thought to fully develop into becoming an action. A friend of mine illustrates this principle with the saying, "If you don't want to go to Minneapolis, don't get on that bus." In short, if you want to end up at a more positive destination, deal with the temptation early on *but* remember the "dealing with it" is not sin in itself; it is the spiritual battle that takes place for our choices.

Character Assassination

The same principle is being portrayed in Matthew 5:21-22 where Jesus speaks of those who murder as "being subject to judgment" and then continues to connect judgment to being angry with others as well as to using derogatory language toward them. Our actions stem from the things we nurture in our hearts. Chapter 5 is showing us a continuum of steps between what happens in the heart and what ends up in our actions. With regard to anger and murder there are a series of steps being shown to us. Anger that is unresolved can lead to speaking badly of the person with whom we are angry. This, in turn, can lead to "character assassination" as we continue to use more and more critical and condemning words about them. The more that we step in the direction of hatred toward the person, the closer we can come to actually harming the individual. Guard the heart, therefore, from such contaminating thoughts taking up residence there so that one can continue to enjoy the wellspring of life.

Festering Wounds

Let's take the previous thought a bit farther and apply it to where we live. Say, for example, that someone has badly hurt you in some way and the memory of this hurt has remained in your heart. You would like to forget it but it never goes away. In fact, it seems that you rehearse it quite often in your mind or expend quite a bit of energy trying *not* to think about it. What happens from there? You probably already know. We tend to let the wound fester to the point where we have said some pretty bad things about the person either right out loud or to ourselves and continue to feel miserable as a result.

If there has been no recognition of the hurt by the other person, we might even have by now garnered enough people in our lives that we have told the story to who also have a deep resentment toward the person. Some might even try to harm them in some way on our behalf—verbally, financially, or even physically. See how what is in our hearts needs to be healed not only for us to feel better, but also to keep us from perpetuating pain on others. Another friend of mine uses the phrase, "We must be careful in fighting dragons that we don't become one ourselves." Wise words indeed.

Forgiving Ourselves

But let's go even one step farther because sometimes the one who needs our forgiveness is . . . us. All of us have things that we are not proud of and may be very ashamed of if these things became public record. Some of these were not of our making yet we carry shame-based stories with us in our hearts that poison the wellsprings of our lives. We try to bury these memories and discover time and again that things that are alive do not stay buried long—they kick and scratch their way to the surface. The wounds of our hearts may not end up in actions where we purposely try to harm others or ourselves, but both can happen.

Possibly there was physical abuse in one's past and as that open wound of the heart spews out stories about ourselves, others, and life itself, we end up acting in self-destructive ways that alienate us from the very ones that we so desperately desire to share intimacy with. Or maybe it's not so much associated with such traumatic events as abuse; maybe it's something that we have done for which we just cannot seem to experience self-forgiveness.

"Stupid Phase"

I've often said that we all go through a "stupid phase" in life where, when we look back on it, say to ourselves "What was I thinking?" Only we realize that we weren't really thinking things through very well at all and the actions that we did were a result of that. Please note that I do not use the phrase "stupid phase" in a derogatory way but rather in the sense of "stupid" having connection to the word "stupor" or things we did as if we were in a stupor at the time.

This doesn't mean that we don't live with the consequences of these behaviors or that they are "okay" but rather that they do not define us today. A quick example are those people I've counseled who have shared with me some things they did in their adolescent or young adult years that they wish they could erase from their memories. They feel so ashamed of these past actions and yet continue to believe in their hearts that because they did _____ at some point in their lives that they are *still* that person today.

The Stories of Our Hearts Guide Our Lives

In our woundedness we create ways of perceiving the world around us that seem to perpetuate our isolation from others. We construct ways of thinking and acting that are incongruent with who we want to be in Christ. The stories that we devise about ourselves, others, and God seem at odds with a grace-filled existence and yet serve as a guide for daily living far below who God has created us to be. We develop a narrowed focus and limited understanding of what lies beyond our daily existence in our Grace Saturated Narrative spoken of later in this book.

Henri Nouwen wrote, "Our pains and joys, our feelings of grief and satisfaction, are not simply dependent on the events of our lives, but also, and even more so, *on the ways we remember these events*" (*Living Reminder*, p. 19). He continued, "It is no exaggeration to say that *the suffering we most frequently encounter . . . is a suffering of memories . . . These memories wound because they are often deeply hidden in the center of our being and very hard to reach*" (p. 21).

The Way I Remember It

Someone once said that we don't live with the facts of our lives, we live with the stories we tell ourselves about these facts. This does not diminish the painful reality of what occurred in our lives at all for these events have left a number of us feeling as dazed and stunned as Dorothy landing in the foreign land of Oz. It does, however, give us hope that can free us from the pain that lingers on in our hearts.

My first little dog Katy, a Yorkshire Terrier, couldn't have been 11 pounds dripping wet at her heaviest point in life. A chain link fence separated my yard from the neighbor who lived behind me but allowed Katy to see the entire yard. One day my neighbor had her son's new Doberman puppy with her as she did some yard work. The puppy, curious as puppies are, came over to the fence. Katy spotted the pup and ran full-speed toward the fence while barking ferociously. She wouldn't have hurt the puppy but the Doberman didn't know that, got scared, and ran to the back door of the neighbor's house. In the weeks and months that followed, the Doberman grew into a massive dog that was many times the size of Katy. When this adult Doberman came to visit, Katy still rushed toward the fence and the dog ran to the back door *as if it was still a pup!* However dogs remember things, this one had a memory of Katy as being big and ferocious; a memory that discarded the reality of how big it had grown to become.

Our memories can act in a similar way. Whatever it was in our past that hurt, scared, embarrassed, victimized, or otherwise harmed us no longer is happening today *except* in our memories and the residual effects of these events. Memories make up the stories of our lives and are what we tell ourselves consciously and unconsciously throughout the day.

Tell Me a Story

We organize our lives through the stories we tell ourselves. This is the way humans make sense of the world in which we live. Nichols and Schwartz (2006) noted, "Life is complicated, so we find ways to explain it. These explanations, the stories we tell ourselves, organize our experience and shape our behavior" (p. 337). One can readily see that the story we tell ourselves is of utmost importance to our health and well-being . . . or the lack of it.

Our hearts are the container of all our stories—pleasant stories, painful stories, and everything in between. A narrative is the way we talk to ourselves about life on a deeper level than simply thinking about life. Our life narratives not only contain the events of our lives but the many stories we tell ourselves about these events and our part and place within them. This is the reason I refer to the heart as "Narrative Central" for it is the place where we tell ourselves the stories in a way that helps or hinders us from functioning optimally in life.

As a professional counselor I've heard many people's stories. As I listen intently to the facts of what occurred in their lives, I also listen for the stories that have developed into the narrative that they live by. There are so many kinds, or genres, of stories that a book could be written on this alone. Let me share just a few of the more common ones I've come across.

Self stories never develop in a vacuum but are always created in relationship with others. How you and I view ourselves is comprised of a variety of data gleaned from the interactions we've had or missed out on with others and the interpretation of what they say about us. If, for example, you were always chosen last for a team when growing up you have developed some story about yourself that affects you into adulthood. Wondering if others really want us around or if others would really rather have someone else can be a result of letting this kind of story go unchallenged.

Self stories can also be the result of what we've been told early on by powerful people in our lives. Someone once wisely noted that the "you" statements of childhood become the "I" statements of adulthood. For example, if you were told that you were stupid, a nuisance, or some other negative thing when growing up, you likely will have a story of being stupid, a nuisance, or some other negative thing into adulthood. The difference is that these stories, since we've rehearsed them over and over again throughout life, have become as easy to wear as our most broken-in jeans but so far short of who others may see us as being today.

> *A Moment for Reflection.* Take a few moments to reflect on what "you statements" came into your life early on. In what ways have these developed into the "I" statements of your adult life? At what cost?

You Feeling Okay?

There is great formative power in the words of others. Who among us hasn't experienced someone saying, "Do you feel well? You look a bit pale" and it not causing us to think for a second if indeed we are feeling well. Such words can have us notice the warmth of our foreheads and question whether a fever is forming. Multiply this many times over and we can begin to feel the power of parental pronouncements about us.

Some of the parental pronouncements are real blessings to us. "You can do it" spoken by a parent to their child can become internalized to the point where we have confidence to try different things in life. Parental pronouncements can be more curse-like in nature to us as well. "What is wrong with you?" and "Why can't you be more like . . . " can create an inner narrative of there being something wrong with us.

Deficit stories. As just noted, when we come to see what we're lacking from the perspective of others, we tend to develop an approach to life wherein we cannot seem to see past our faults. We somehow think that if we can just "get it right" that somehow *we will be right* but find we can never rid ourselves of the feelings of being deficient no matter how much we achieve.

Deficit stories focus on the me that *should be* for acceptance and overlooks the *me that is* and the numerous qualities that go unnoticed by me. These positive qualities readily get dismissed as not counting since they *should* be there anyway. Deficit stories always have a "should" statement in them and all "should" statements leave us feeling short of our goal.

This leads to another genre: *guilt and shame stories.* When we set unrealistic goals for ourselves that we hold to as being realistic, we always fail. Failing to achieve what I think I should be leaves me feeling ashamed and guilty. After all, everybody knows I should have been or done this or that and I'm not. A counseling lead I often use with clients suffering from this genre of stories is "Says who?" After a time of reflection my clients will be able to boil it down to someone having told them this and it has remained unchallenged over the years until I asked them to examine the truth of such expectations.

Guilt and shame stories also get developed when we feel like we're the only one who struggles in a particular area. This is where one of the powerfully therapeutic qualities of a group—a sense of universality—can be of great help. The sense of universality happens when we share what we believe to have been only experienced by us and discover that others have struggled similarly. This helps us to drop our guard a bit and feel less like an anomaly and more like a normal human being.

I recall leading a group for adolescent clients when the concept of universality became a reality for one of the members of the group. As one young woman shared her story of struggling to stay on the medication she was taking for depression I could tell that one of the young men in the group was listening with rapt attention. When she finished he said, "I thought I was the only one" and told her how he felt better just knowing someone else was going through what he was and finding strength and support from the group.

God stories is the genre we develop in regard to how God sees us and how we see God. For example, some clients have come in stating, "God hates me. I just know it!" When we sat down and tried to unpack that story a bit, I quickly discovered that the client's beliefs *about* God were treated as though they were *actually how God is*. These God stories are referred to as the *God concept* and discussed more fully in a later chapter. Suffice it to say for now that such stories can be powerful in how one approaches or removes oneself from God in living out one's life.

Body stories are the type that can keep us from enjoying the bodies we live in. Body stories also develop very early in life and can develop into anything from dissatisfaction with how we look to loathing our appearance. Negative body stories can develop out of the lessons we are taught and caught by parents and other powerful figures in our lives. For example, some parents who over-react to catching their children "playing doctor" or touching themselves in the genital area can set the stage for body stories that sexuality is bad and much shame can come as a result of this belief.

Childhood sexual abuse often sets the stage for body stories that need to be healed. For some, all forms of sexual expression are feared and can be seen as painful and disgusting. This can rob the person from ever enjoying their body, even with the person they marry. For others, the body story becomes one in which the person has learned to please others with their body and found it is a way of being accepted. There is a detachment then between the body and the person who lives in it in that the person feels they are only loved and accepted when they are sexual.

Traumatic stories often are told in the counselor's office and can be so powerful in how they color a person's view of life. Traumatic events and the stories we tell ourselves about them leave one feeling raw and vulnerable and can lead a person into viewing the world as being a very unsafe place. We are wounded by the initial events and often further wounded by the stories we develop about the trauma.

In counseling a woman in her early 40s for some sexual abuse she had suffered as a very young child I recall vividly her saying, "I still can't figure out what *I did to cause him to do such a thing*." She was two years old when the victimization took place and some 30 plus years later not only suffered from what the abuse did to her but also from the story she developed about the abuse; that she was somehow responsible for being abused. As we counseled together she not only was able to find healing from what happened but also from what she told herself about the painful events.

Whenever we go through painful events in life we try to make sense of them. It's a process called *meaning making* and entails developing a story to answer the *why questions* that arise from what has happened. We often look for reasons why things happen out of a belief that this is an ordered world in which we live (this also can intersect with the God stories we tell ourselves). Unfortunately, sometimes the "reasons" we come up with only give temporary relief and long-term pain.

As a pastor and chaplain I've been around a number of people who have lost loved ones to death. I've also been privy to hearing a number of stories by surviving family members who share what others have told them as to possible reasons the person died (this is especially true in situations that seemingly make no sense at all). At best, the "reasons" people give for such losses *give the person saying them* a sense of comfort that the world *makes sense* and, at worst, further wounds the ones who have lost the loved one.

An example of this was an article I read many years ago that spoke of the death of a well-known recording artist. In the article the author wrote something to the effect that "heaven must have needed a good tenor" for a reason the person died tragically at a young age. On the surface this may sound very flattering to the person who died. After all, think of all the people who have gone before us and how many tenors there are among them. This person must *really* have been a great tenor (and he was by the way). However, if I am the family members this comfort may have a very short shelf life. Questions like, "Why did God take my husband for his heavenly choir? Doesn't God have enough tenors by now?" or "He wasn't just a tenor, he was the love of my life. Why did God take him?" could easily be the questions that flow from the heart of loss.

Making meaning is a way of making sense of what has happened to us and we need to be very careful of coming up too quickly with simple answers to complex questions in life. The developing of stories about life includes how we interpret the events and, as is noted above, shapes how we think, feel, and act. Be it in the counseling office or across the table from a friend, we work with meaning and believe that the meaning of life events comes from the stories people tell themselves and each other about those events.

Healing Memories, Healing Stories

We all enter adulthood with our "book bags" packed with life stories. Some of these stories need real healing for us ever to reach the potential God has in mind for us but all of us have stories needing a healthy adjustment since stories are not static, they move us toward interpreting our present interactions (i.e., the narrative we live by). Nichols and Schwartz (2006) tell us that "when memory speaks it tells a 'narrative truth,' which comes to have more influence than 'historical truth'"(p. 350). *How* we tell our stories to ourselves and others tends to create how we experience life as a result of our stories about the facts of our lives to date.

The Difficult Work of Editing Our Stories

In his book *Reaching for the Invisible God: What Can We Expect to Find?*, Yancey wrote a line that stood out to me regarding the hard work of changing how we interpret life. "I live in daily awareness of how much easier it is to edit a book than edit a life" (p. 195). It is hard work that requires daily attention and energy if we are to find the courage to open up our hearts to attain healing in the depths of our souls.

The tough work of editing old narratives is well worth it however for only as we approach life from this new perspective will we experience living like never before. One of the first tasks in accomplishing this goal is to gain a new understanding about problems. Concurrently we need to understand and apply new levels of grace to the fibers of our being. Since we did not develop closed hearts in a relational vacuum, we're also in need of finding Grace-Saturated People who can help in the process. Finally, we'll need to "come home" to being the person God created us to be long before we ever existed physically. Are you ready to begin this journey? Let's go!

4

___

The Problem with Problems—
A New Way of Approaching Change

A COLLEAGUE OF MINE has been known to say to incoming classes of counseling students, "I've got stuff, you've got stuff, all God's children got stuff" as a way of clearing away any misconceptions that any of us are perfect or should be. This helps us to lower our guards and face ourselves *as we are* rather than how we think we *should be* so that we can make progress toward what God has designed us to be. In other words, giving up on perfection allows us to have the energy to work on improvement that was previously used to maintain an illusion of having it all together. It reminds me of when I was young and our family would go to the lake. Sometimes as kids we would throw a beach ball back and forth as we played in the waves. Occasionally one of us would hide the ball from others by submerging it underwater. Holding it underwater involved some effort and skill. Effort to keep it pushed under water when it naturally exerted pressure to surface and skill to keep a hand on it while the currents and waves jostled it around. Keeping the beach ball underwater took energy that could be used for other things (such as swimming) as well as the loss of mobility (moving would surely allow the beach ball to escape). Pretending we're "okay" when we're not or that we've got it together when we don't takes energy and skill as well.

This is a good place for us to start. None of us is perfect nor will we ever be in this lifetime and so we humbly must accept our humanity and work toward learning how to become more like Christ as we struggle to "put off our old selves and put on the new" as Scripture states. As noted in earlier chapters, we live in a world that is not operating to the capacity of what God had created it for and so it is more realistic to accept the fact that as long as we're human, we will contend with problems of various kinds—some of our own making.

Understanding Problems

The problem with problems is that we don't have a proper understanding of them. That leads to even more problems trying to solve what we don't understand. Let me explain. Too often we come up with simple answers for very complex issues and feel frustrated when our "solutions" don't "fix it" in self and others. We have been so enculturated with quick fixes and easy solutions that it fosters more hiding behaviors when we seemingly cannot fix our problems no matter how many times we try. This leaves us feeling like there must be something wrong with us since what apparently works for others isn't working.

"Just Stop It!"

Bob Newhart did a comedy skit on *MadTV* where he played the role of a psychologist none of us would want to seek out for help. For those of us who grew up watching the "Bob Newhart Show" where his character was a kind, warm psychologist, this was a classic parody. How this applies to what I am saying is that the comedy skit showed a troubled young woman coming to the psychologist for help with excessive worries and fears that she could not overcome. She had apparently been to other mental health professionals by some of the things she said and now sought out his help. The psychologist's advice to her was "Just stop it!" as if it was that easy. Too often those who don't understand problems in life can say similar things to those who struggle and those of us who struggle feel guilt, shame, frustration, and anger as we find ourselves grappling with the same problem over and over again.

M. Scott Peck (1978) in one of his early works made a very short but poignant statement: "Life is difficult." He then went on to say that once we accept the fact that life is difficult, it isn't quite as difficult anymore. This really is a starting point for each of us. Life truly is difficult as opposed to expecting it to be easy or easily remedied. Each day it seems that we come to a closer understanding of new intricacies of problems that we as human beings deal with and seek to help hurting individuals, couples, and families function more healthily. Thankfully we are a far cry away from drilling holes in people's heads to let evil spirits out and have given up draining blood from people in an attempt to cure them of difficulties. Yet, we have not fully arrived at understanding the complexities of problems and so at times we are not very gracious to one another as we struggle.

"Be Nice to Everyone for Everyone's Life is Hard"

When I was in my graduate training in counseling I gained permission to sit in on a support group for people who had family members who were dealing with major psychiatric disorders such as schizophrenia. These kind and gracious individuals shared their joys and sorrows with one another who understood their world of everyday interactions because many others in their lives just did not understand. Something from that meeting stood out in my mind more than anything else I heard that evening. It was a simple sentence, written on the chalkboard prior to anyone coming to the group. The words were simply, "Be nice to everyone for everyone's life is hard." I read the sentence before the group began and as members shared their experiences; I knew on a much deeper level why that statement was so important. A starting place for us, then, is to offer grace and mercy to everyone who struggles with problems *including ourselves*.

Grace!

Life indeed is difficult and full of twists and turns. *Grace*. We've all made bad decisions along the way and some of us are still dealing with the consequences of these decisions. *Grace*. Some of us are making and will make decisions in the present and very near future that add to, rather than detract from, our problem base. *Grace*. Many of us have family members and friends who will be doing the same. *Grace*. You see, grace needs to be offered to others and us each and every day. Does this mean that we should simply accept our problems as the stuff of life and quit trying to change? Absolutely not. We need to keep working on becoming more healthy and whole but realize that it is a process that takes time and humility, often *much* time and humility.

All of us need grace for our past, present, and future. We need to embrace the fact that we surely can never find the limits of God's love—the height, depth, and width that Scripture speaks of—and grace no matter how far we travel from "home." Does this give license to "travel" into whatever we desire? No. It does give us healing from the roadside hazards we all experience in the journeys that we are on. I love the earthiness of some of the writings and confessions of the past. One line comes to mind from one liturgy that honestly proclaims "I have not loved God with my whole heart or my neighbor as myself" and seeks forgiveness for such wanderings of the heart. God's grace meets us there in our humility.

> *A Moment for Reflection.* I would encourage you to stop and ask yourself the following question: How rich and efficacious is the blood of Jesus Christ? Is it rich enough to cover only past sins and failings or does it have the power to help us learn how to say "no" to ungodliness (Titus Chapter 2 referred to earlier in this book)? Is it rich and deep enough to heal from failings that we are making currently or on the very verge of committing? If the answer is anything less than a resounding "Yes!" then may I ask what more God needs to do to cover for future sins? For further thought, read the first chapter of First John, especially verse 9. At this point I can almost hear the critics saying, "He's giving permission to sin! Don't listen to him." Nothing could be farther from the truth. In humility, however, I recognize that we, like the "sinner" in Jesus' story of the Publican and the sinner in the Gospels, know we have sinned and need his forgiveness on a daily basis.

Thick Grace Not "Cheap Grace"

This is not some "thin" version of grace or a cheap grace, this is costly grace that is more rich and deep and "thick" than we can imagine. I recently heard a prominent Christian leader claim that we need the thick blood of Christ, not the thin "Kool-Aid" version that many live by. I agree wholeheartedly with him as it relates to the grace of Christ afforded by his very rich sacrifice.

Problems, then, come along with living and so we must humbly accept that fact and find grace to help us in dealing with them in ourselves and others. We need to also understand that for many problems, there is a connection of nature and nurture so why not err on the side of grace by treating all people as Christ would—compassionately. In other words, let's try listening to understand the person and their struggle so as to compassionately respond.

Who Wants Problems?

Imagine with me for a moment that newborn babies could talk. If this were possible, do you think the first words they would say would be something like, "Yippee, I'm born! Now, where can I find my share of problems?" Ridiculous. Not only is it ridiculous to think a newborn baby could speak in such a way, it is *equally ridiculous* to think that anyone coming into the world would desire to have problems. And yet, it seems that the ways we treat others and ourselves at times would indicate that we might think some people really do want problems. How so? Here's how. We oftentimes treat people as if they were the problem they are dealing with. Persons and the problems they struggle with are *not* synonymous and yet it is far too easy to say "they must want to be that way" or, as in some cases in counseling, one member of the family is the "identified patient" or the one *with the problem*. It is time we gain a different view of problems so that we can have more success in dealing with them and more connection with others as we do.

Problems Are the Real Problem

In my counseling of others over the years, I have found that we can make so much better progress when we view problems for what they are—problems to be dealt with—and not equate them with the person being counseled. To help make this a bit clearer, let me share an example. When I first meet with a couple for marriage counseling, they often come in emotionally and relationally battered and bruised. Problems have beaten them both up and coming to counseling can often be the second to the last professional they are wishing to consult with, the final one being a lawyer. As the couple sits down and begins to unpack the reasons for their conflict, I hear stories of hurt and pain, misunderstanding and devaluing, hope turned to despair. Couples in crisis often have their defenses up fearing that they will be further blamed by their partner for where they find themselves at this juncture in their relationship.

At this point some counselors might try to focus on resolving problems, teaching new skills such as communication and conflict management skills, even helping the couple see how issues from their families of origin (a fancy way of saying "the families in which we grew up") affected their situation now. These can all be very fruitful approaches to take at some point in the counseling process but I find we need to start not with the problems themselves but rather with the couple dealing with the problems; the couple distinct from the problems they are dealing with. Here's how. I listen to the problems as the couple describes them but from the beginning speak of the problems as something separate from the persons experiencing them. I hear things like "I don't feel like he hears what I care about" and respond by saying something like "So, you feel he's having a hard time hearing what's important to you. For some reason it seems like the one who used to hear your heart now can't hear you anymore. Something makes it difficult for him to hear you." Or I might hear "I don't feel like she cares whether I even exist anymore" to which I might reply, "You feel that somehow your existence is not noticed. Like something has blinded the one you've been with so that she has lost sight of you and you don't like how that feels."

Broken Spokes

Often I will follow up by using the example of two travelers on a cross-country trip from where they met to where they want to be. Somewhat like the early settlers they are traveling in a covered wagon and on this day they have encountered a breakdown due to one of the wheels needing repair. I ask the couple to imagine a wagon wheel between them where some of its spokes are damaged or broken. I let them know that the spokes nearest them are the only ones they can repair and to leave those closest to their partner for them to repair without "help" unless they are requesting it. Why do I do this? Because as any beginning marriage counselor knows, the client isn't either of those sitting in front of me, the *client is the relationship*—the thing that occurs between them. Similar to this, I see the couple dealing with problems (i.e., the broken spokes I mentioned earlier) that are distinct from the persons being affected by them. Think about it for a moment: is it easier for a person to deal with a problem than to *be* the problem? Also, doesn't it bring two people who love each other closer together when they are battling a problem rather than battling a person struggling with a problem?

Labeling Problems

Chosing couples' counseling as the example helps lay a foundation for understanding problems with which individuals and entire families deal. Using the two examples noted above I can easily label these problems as "hearing loss" and "distraction" as the troubles that are negatively affecting two people who care for each other deeply or *cared* deeply at one time for each other before these problems robbed them of such care. As we will look at a bit later in this chapter, when a person is able to label a problem affecting their relationship at least two positive things happen. First, they are able to separate the person from the problem they are encountering. This makes it so much easier to deal with because I can work on a problem. I can't work on a problem if *I am the problem*. So if the problem is somehow so enmeshed with my person that *I* will never be seen as separate from the problems that have plagued me then I am doomed.

A second positive thing that happens is that the partner often can garner the strength to stand alongside the other as they work to overcome the problem. In other words, when a person can see that a problem is beating up the one they care for and it is attacking their relationship, it turns the attention and energy toward the problem. Anger can then be directed away from the other partner and towards the problem with which their partner has been struggling. I have seen so much positive growth in relationships when the couple pulls together in a united front against the problems they previously saw as being somehow resident in the fiber of the other person's being.

Problems Have Tricks and Tactics

A few bits of helpful information on the nature of problems need to be shared here because problems are sneaky in how they attack people. First of all we need to know that *problems are masters of camouflage* and have an innate ability to affix themselves so tightly to people that it takes skill in training oneself to see the problem as separate from the person. "My son is so rebellious!" shows that we haven't acquired the skill of separating persons from problems yet; "My son is struggling with rebellion's invitations towards misconduct" shows a better understanding of a loved one battling a problem.

Problems often run in packs, feeding off of each other. Using the example above of the son who is struggling with rebellion, I often see that others in the family are fighting against their own problems that have aligned themselves with the one the young man is dealing. For example, the young man's parents may be battling with fear of letting the son start making life choices which can add to the intensity of the son's struggle. Here's how: the son may be dealing with both the hormonal changes that come in adolescence at the same time that he's learning how to take over the reins of his life. This can accentuate the tone and intensity of responses. At the same time as he is learning to take control of his own decisions, his parent's fear of loosening their grip on the reins of the young man's life and how that might play out comes into play. So, if we could personify these problems (spoken of later in this chapter), it would go something like this. The parent wants to loosen their grip on their son's decision-making yet fear whispers in their ear, "You know, if he makes a bad decision it could ruin his future chances at college and a career." Listening to fear causes the parent to hold onto the reins a bit too tightly. Sensing this, the son can hear rebellion tempting him to give a harsh response and possibly slam a door or two to punctuate it. And so two problems collide into an unhealthy and unsatisfying relationship between the son and his parent(s).

To this point I have not said much about our responsibility in dealing with problems and some may wonder if I am saying that we share no responsibility for the results of cooperating with problems. Nothing could be farther from the truth. *Problems are deceptive and we are drawn into cooperating with them* and when we do, everyone suffers. I am reminded of the temptation process outlined in the first chapter of the book of James. It shows that what starts as desire leads to action that leads to an unwanted outcome. So it is true that we are tempted to go along with (cooperate) with the enticement of a problem. When we do cooperate with the problem, we find that it takes us to a place where we did not want to be. Problems seem to have great skill in persuasiveness in their promise of some positive outcome in "buying their product" so to speak.

"BAD"

An acronym that I've used for years to describe the process of being drawn into unhealthy choices is the word "BAD." The "B" represents the early phase of being tempted into cooperating with problems and stands for "Beckons." Problems are sneaky and, like the Sirens of mythological lore, call out to us to come close only to find later that we were drawn into a rocky shoreline. So problems beckon us to cooperate with them, somehow promising a positive outcome for such cooperation. Truth in advertising? Not a chance with problems! They have the corner on the market in the bait and switch approach—"baited" into believing in a good outcome with the payoff "switched" to an unsatisfying, and sometimes devastating, result.

The letter "A" in my acronym represents "Ambush" and has to do with the immediate and far-reaching consequences of having cooperated with a problem. Often it begins with feeling ambushed by guilt for having given in and beginning to see the negative results. For example, the person struggling to stay clear of giving in to alcoholism's "beckoning." For such a person to take a drink or visit an old, familiar place they used to enjoy frequenting, the biting feeling of guilt is standing nearby should they cooperate with such beckoning. Something to take note of is that problems vary in their intensity and complexity. Alcoholism and other forms of addiction are among the more intense and complex problems with which people deal.

Often people are poignantly aware of the first two letters of the acronym but the third one ties into another bit of information on problems that we need to know. The "D" represents "Downplays" and as it applies here, *problems tempt us to disregard or downplay times of success over them.* Why? Because problems are sneaky and don't want us to believe we can ever have the upper hand. The truth is that we do not cooperate with problems 24/7. There are times where we make decisions and choices that run contrary to the problems with which we are wrestling. Problems want us to focus on failures not successes as if success is equivalent to never having a failure. Problems want us to say to ourselves, "Hey, even a stopped clock is right twice a day. So you didn't give in to [problem] just now, big deal. You were just lucky!"

Problems seem to know who is most susceptible to them. Remember, everyone struggles in one way or another and so we need to realize that it's not that we alone are struggling with a problem; it's that we often feel that our problem is more unique, and therefore troublesome, than those experienced by others. For example, if one is struggling with alcoholism one might be tempted to say, "Why do I have this problem when other people I know who've battled alcoholism are doing better than me?" or "Why do I have this problem that is so difficult to overcome when others seem to deal with smaller ones. What's wrong with me?" The truth is, again, that we all struggle with something in life and each of us seems to be more susceptible to one genre of problems or another.

In the counseling world, the discussion over "nature versus nurture" continues to exist. In other words, when we look at problems that people encounter, the question is how much of the problem is related to nature, the genetic inclination toward the problem, and how much of the problem is due to how we were raised, the nurture aspect. In many cases the answer is that it is some combination of nature and nurture.

Faulty Emotional Fire Alarms

Anxiety is an example of a problem experienced by many with some people tending to struggle more with it than others. We are still discovering new things about brain chemistry and connections to being susceptible to becoming overly anxious (nature) but adding to this is how these same people have learned (nurture) to live.

One extreme form of anxiety is called a panic attack. When someone has a panic attack, it is similar to having a faulty emotional fire alarm. Our nervous system reacts as if that fire alarm has been pulled and we experience the emotional response we would have *if* there were a real danger. Some emotional responses are so strong that people end up in emergency rooms thinking they are having a heart attack. For others, the after-effects of such an attack are nearly as strong. One after-effect is anxiety over having another panic attack. This can cause the person to not want to leave the security of their home for fear of another attack.

One way of understanding this after-effect is to think of a time you have gotten sick after having a certain food or beverage. Remember how long it took you to have that food or beverage again? I recall an instance when at a new restaurant I ordered a hot cup of Chinese almond milk. It was so good that I ordered a second cup along with my meal. Later that evening the richness of the meal was more than my system could handle and I became ill. After-effect? You guessed it; I couldn't have another Chinese almond milk (or even think the word "almond") for a long time. Why? My mind had determined that the Chinese almond milk was the reason I got sick and therefore made me queasy every time I thought about anything "almond."

Using my little story of Chinese almond milk, sometimes the "nurture" element of problems is how we have chosen to believe and act as a result of having experienced a problem. Back to panic attacks, sometimes people who experience them have both a genetic sensitivity towards anxiety and have learned to be anxious in how they approach life. This leads to a final thought about the tricks and strategies that problems have. It seems that *some problems run in families.*

There is a Scripture passage that goes something like this, "The sins of the fathers are visited upon their children and children's children." For some people I've spoken to, this passage of Scripture seems to say that we are now somehow responsible for what our parents and grandparents did. This is not what is being said. The message of these verses is that sometimes the effects of what others have done affect us today. Most all of us would agree that on a physical dimension this is true. For example, alcohol use during pregnancy can potentially negatively impact a baby's life and once the child is born, the problems may be life-long. In this case the choices of the mother have long-lasting implications for the child.

Bulls-Eye!

The passage of Scripture speaks more to the nurture aspect. One definition of "sin" is "missing the mark." When an archer misses the mark, they miss the bulls-eye or maybe the target altogether! Using archery as an example, "archers" raised each of us and some were not very good at hitting the bulls-eye. When our grandparents raised our parents, if they were "missing the mark" in some area, they passed along that "skill" to our parents who, in turn, passed that along to us. Maybe "missing the mark" in one family was how to deal with conflict, whereas in another it is how to parent children. See what I mean? Some families have learned poor life archery skills and, like one definition of insanity goes, keep doing the same thing over and over but expect a different result.

Problems that have run in families for generations resist being changed. A person I once worked with in counseling came from a family where alcohol was abused. This person experienced the effects of this problem and no longer wanted to live this way and yet wanted to have an ongoing relationship with her family. The problem of alcohol abuse in the family made it difficult for her to attend family gatherings, as there was always the pressure to change her opinion and "loosen up" some. My client had seen the devastation that alcohol abuse had caused the family in the past and no longer wanted this form of "missing the mark" to be characteristic of her life nor did she want this modeled to her children.

Problems Come in a Variety of Forms

Problems we deal with present themselves in a variety of ways—behavioral, emotional, cognitive (including both "quick" thoughts and deep narratives), and relational. Behavioral problems can be understood as those things that we *do* or *fail to do* that have negative consequences. Things such as anger outbursts, defiant behavior, addictions to various things, nagging, and verbal tirades fit into this category. Emotional problems are those involving our feelings that are causing us pain. Emotions such as excessive anxiety, rage, guilt, and depression are among the culprits.

Problems of the cognitive kind include how we interpret life and what we tell ourselves about others, self, and life events. These involve what I've termed "quick thoughts" and "deep narratives." "Quick thoughts" are those that seemingly come so automatically that we almost don't even notice thinking them. For example, if someone were to cut you off on the highway and your immediate thought is "Jerk!" I would classify this as a "quick thought" problem.

"Deep narratives" are thoughts that seem to be pervasive as we go throughout life and are often rooted in our painful histories. Somewhat like a computer operating system, deep narratives are the "operating system" we have developed. For example, someone who feels worthless despite all evidence that they are a person of great worth to God and others is likely struggling from an inner storyline that was painfully developed in the past. Problems in relationships are those difficulties that happen when one or more people seek to relate but find this very difficult, and even painful, to do. As noted earlier, life is complex and so are the problems that we deal with. In truth, most problems contain some negative interplay of behaviors, emotions, quick thoughts, deep narratives, and/or relationships.

Time Does Not Heal All Wounds

Problems occur within three time frames: past, present and future. As human beings we have the God-given capacity to live within any of the time frames mentioned. For example, as I sit here at my keyboard, I can reflect upon the Egg McMuffin breakfast I had a few hours ago (past), the feel of the keyboard on my fingertips (present), or yard work I have to do when I get home tonight (future). Problems, however, do not take such positive or neutral forms as I just wrote. Problems of the past include regrets, shame, guilt, unforgiveness, and the like.

Something to take note of is that unforgiveness lets those who have hurt you live rent-free in your head and heart. How so? Whenever we harbor bitterness and unforgiveness, the person or persons who have hurt us are with us constantly in thought and emotion. They show up when we're alone remind us of the wrongs done. They appear in our dreams as our minds try to make sense of what has happened. They invite themselves into our conversations which abruptly changing our moments of happiness into emotions we'd prefer not to have. It's as if they are sitting at our dining room table and neither pay for the meal they are ruining or the time spent in our homes.

The old saying that "time heals all wounds" isn't really true. Generally speaking, time only makes untreated wounds become old wounds that still very much hurt. Problems in the present are those things happening right now in one or more of the problem areas noted above. Some of these include negatively reading into the statements of others, quick-tempered statements, and binge eating.

The "What If Neighborhood"

Problems of the future concern what we fear will happen but has not yet occurred. Such problems live in what I term the "What If Neighborhood." The "What If Neighborhood" houses all of our "what if" statements that cause us anxiety. We've all visited this neighborhood before when we say things to ourselves like, "*What if* I don't have enough money to make my house payment?" or "*What if* I lose my job? How will I survive?" or even "*What if* my son/daughter marries the wrong person?" The result of visiting the "What If Neighborhood" is anxiety, worry, and fear. But it is *so* inviting at times to visit this neighborhood, isn't it? I've even told people that the "What If Neighborhood" has such inviting brochures that make it seem like the place to visit but we always get emotionally "mugged" when we visit.

Problems not only occur in various time frames, they come in a variety of strengths as well.

Problem Strength

The strength of any problem may range from mild to severe thus necessitating differing levels of intervention. Some of the problems we encounter need very little attention to be managed well. For example, some problems are ameliorated by gaining knowledge that we had not possessed before. Books and seminars can serve well here. Other problems are of the variety that cause deep and lasting wounds. All problems create difficulties for us but it seems that some are so strong that, left unaddressed, they can severely cripple or destroy us and the relationships we have. Again, we need to treat one another with kindness for everyone's life is difficult in varying degrees.

Personifying Problems

As I have been saying so far, for us to deal differently with problems we need to envision them differently. Problems need to not only be separated from the people who are suffering from them but I also find that personifying problems helps us deal more effectively with them. Think for a moment about any problem that you have dealt with or are currently struggling to overcome. Doesn't it seem like you're being bullied and pushed around by it at times? Like some bully that you'd like to be rid of? Or, sometimes problems are like thieves taking away things in life that we enjoy. At other times problems can whisper in our ears some really nasty things about us. Problems, then, need not only be labeled appropriately but also personifying them helps us in approaching them.

In counseling sessions I will often ask clients to imagine their problem as sitting in a chair across the room from them. Then I will ask my client what the problem has been doing to them and stealing from them. For example, when a client is dealing with depression, oftentimes they feel like "depression" has stolen their enjoyment in life, kept them from going outside much, and has tempted them to think very negatively about themselves and life itself.

The Change Process

So what do we do with this new understanding of problems? I mean, it's great to gain a new vision of what problems are and how they operate but how does that play out in everyday life? This truly is at the crux of the matter isn't it? Since no one really wants problems and yet we struggle with them in life, let's look for a bit about how we can approach problems so that we have mastery over them and not vice versa.

Take a Stance

To begin with, we absolutely, unapologetically, *must* see problems for what they are—problems we deal with that are separate from ourselves. In other words, we cannot allow ourselves to waiver in our belief about what problems are no matter what others try to tell us. The world around us, including people who love us, may or may not agree that the problems we deal with are separate from us and need to be fought like an enemy trying to harm us. We can't change their opinion or belief about problems but we must not waiver in separating the problems we deal with from the person of who we are.

Remember, problems will seek to reinforce that we are the problem as a defense against being discovered. We simply cannot be duped into believing that. For example, others might label someone who struggles with quick thoughts that produce sharp responses as a "hothead." Or the person who struggles with addictive behavior often gets the "addict" designation. And even some who should know better can unfortunately label even the person who deals with borderline personality disorder as "borderline." We are not *hotheads*, *addicts*, or *borderlines* . . . we are people of immense worth struggling with problems. Never, ever allow yourself to waiver on this point or problems regain a foothold and become even more difficult to overcome.

Name Your Problem

In an article authored by outdoor humorist Patrick McManus was a line that has stuck with me over the years. The scene is a boy traveling at breakneck speed on his bicycle past an older man who calls out to the young man to see where he's going in such a hurry. The boy says something to the effect that he did not know where he was going, to which the older man said, "If you don't know where you're going . . . what's your hurry to get there?" To me this speaks of having a clearly labeled goal to achieve so as not to be exerting a lot of energy without making much progress.

Early on, then, we must name the problem we are dealing with so that we can effectively deal with it. For example, maybe the problem you are dealing with is depression. You can simply name this problem "depression" or, better yet, sit with it for a little bit to come up with a more clearly identifiable name that is customized to your life and circumstances. You could name the problem something like "deep darkness" or, to borrow a term from the book *The Shack*, depression might be named "the great sadness."

Naming the problem helps us see what we are dealing with and where we want to go with it. It also fosters a sense of separateness from the problem so that we can fight against it. In a movie example, *A Beautiful Mind*, the lead character John Nash is dealing with schizophrenia, a major problem that negatively affects thoughts, behaviors, emotions, and relationships. In the film, the problem is personified in three persons that only John Nash can see and interact with. Although this is a fictionalized depiction of what such a disorder is, it serves us well in how we need to deal with problems.

We need to see them as following us around, taunting us at first until we see them for what they are and we take control of our lives again, ignoring the calls and taunts of problems that once ruled us.

Problems as Unemployed Magicians

Our next step is to investigate problems that plague us so that we can figure out what they're up to and how we can overcome them. As long as problems keep us in the dark as to their origin, what they need to survive, and their tactics, we continue to be at risk to fail prey to them. Once we do discover how they thrive, we gain more control. In my mind it's like discovering how magic tricks are done. Before we understand what's going on, we can easily be deceived into thinking that entire buildings can disappear or glamorous assistants are turned into tigers in a cage. Magicians stay employed by keeping their secrets to themselves; problems stay strong by doing the same.

Investigating problems involves us searching out their history so as to understand how and when were they were "born" into our lives. In this way we might discover that the problems we deal with now may have been in our homes growing up and naturally we felt they were "part of the family" even though we don't like them at all. For instance, it's very possible that a person dealing with anxiety was exposed to the anxiety that plagued another family member such as a parent.

We also need to investigate what the problem needs to survive. What exactly does the problem thrive on? Sometimes we discover that problems thrive on secrets and silence. In other words, some problems rely on us to keep silent so they can continue to exist. They whisper things such as, "If you share this with anyone, they'll know how screwed up you are and then they'll leave you. Trust me on this one, no one is as messed up as you, so don't tell anyone!" The truth is, when we share with a trusted other the problem with which we are dealing, it takes a lot of the power away from it. Problems don't want that to *ever* happen.

We need to discover what tricks and tactics problems employ. Gaining such information helps to equip and prepare us to deal successfully with problems. Along with the tactics, we need to learn how problems "talk" to us. Remember, if we personify problems, these problems do indeed elicit conversations within us. For example, when we're struggling with problems what thoughts come to mind that work against us? In other words, what are these problems telling you about you, others, God, life, et cetera?

One more thing we need to discover is finding out how we have overcome the problem in the past. People are more resourceful than they think and no one gives in to problems 24/7. As noted in another chapter, we have many victories over the problems we encounter but for some reason, these don't get counted very often. Why? Because we are living in a society where partial victories are synonymous with failure . . . and problems love such a society as that. Find out how you've beaten the problem at its own game before and if it's something you consciously did, it's likely that will work for you again. If it was by chance that you overcame the problem, still try to figure out how that happened and possibly you can use that more intentionally next time.

Problem Cycle

For a number of problems that we face we can see a predictable pattern or cycle that they use. Simply knowing this will help us to know where we're at in the cycle and make plans to intervene in what might normally be a very slippery slope into giving into the problem's demands. The pattern I refer to can be seen in the following progression—*environment, early warning signs, escalation, escape/event, evaluation and education.*

To begin with, problems tend to find strength in certain *environments* so this is a perfect place to try to seek to "nip them in the bud" so to speak. For example, if I am aware that arguments with my spouse or children happen usually after a very stressful day when I'm tired and suffering from what I call the "Popeye Disorder" (as the cartoon character Popeye the Sailor would say, "I've stands all I can stands and can't stands no more"), I need to do something to deal more positively with the environment that caused the stress that brewed into a vulnerability to cooperate with being surly at home.

Early Warning Signs are usually there if we stop and pay attention to them. Using the example above, what are the early warning signs of someone being vulnerable to giving into arguing? Possibly there is a sense of mild irritation, a sharpness to words that isn't normally there, an "I don't care" attitude brewing, and even aggressive driving. All of these can give signs to us that we need to attend to before the problem uses them to its advantage. Early warning signs alert us to the *Escalation* taking place within us. It is so much easier to stop an avalanche when it is a little snowball starting to pick up speed than it is to intervene later when the growing force is insurmountable. The trick is to develop ways of escaping the escalation rather than hoping something happens along that will break the cycle. It rarely does.

As I write this chapter it's "March Madness" in collegiate basketball. During this time of year there are millions of basketball fans glued to their televisions hoping that their team will become the national champion. Let's say, for example, that you and I were at a friend's apartment watching the championship game and this friend lives on the 15th floor of a high-rise apartment complex. During a break in the game we all quickly grabbed some food from the kitchen but in our haste, someone got the paper napkins too close to the stove. The game goes on and someone notices the smell of smoke and says something. The game is so intense though that no one wants to check the source of the smoke. One of those in attendance jokes, "Hey, if it's bad, we can always use the outside escape ladder." Everyone chuckles but no one budges from the game.

As the game intensifies so does the smell of smoke in the apartment. No one is joking now as plumes of black smoke fill the room and the room catches fire between us and the only way of escape—the outside ladder. If only we would have attended to the couple of burning napkins earlier we wouldn't need to dash through flames and smoke now to escape. As extreme as this example is, the point of it takes place on a regular basis as we face problems. Deal with them as soon as possible before they escalate.

If we have paid attention to and dealt with problems in the environment, noticing early warning signs, and acting on them before they have escalated too far, we will then *Escape* successfully from the problem; if we don't, we experience the *Event* or consequence of the problem winning out. This is where we give in and cooperate with the problem. The next step is where we *Evaluate* what we've done and can either feel good about having overcome the problem's attack or be tempted to feel guilty for having cooperated. This is the "ambush" part of the "BAD" acronym noted earlier in the chapter.

Even when we give into problems and feel badly as a result of it, we have the opportunity to gain more insight into what went wrong in the *Education* phase of the cycle. This is where we look back to see what we could have done differently at a different point in the cycle. As a friend of mine says, "If you don't want to go to Minneapolis, don't get on that bus." We can realize after we've taken such a "bus ride" how it was that we found ourselves boarding it. This way we have a better chance of not getting on board again the next time.

Recruit Support

We are not alone in dealing with whatever problem it is that we're facing. Others have faced these same problems in the past, or are facing them currently, and can serve as both a support and resource. Finding others who deal with similar problems can help us learn new strategies for overcoming the problem and give encouragement to keep up the fight against the problem. Support groups can be great places to find fellow travelers along the path we're walking but you don't have to find a support group, you can develop a supportive group of people you trust.

Oftentimes the first person that we find real support from is one who has traveled this path, but they are not the only ones who can support us. We need to discover people of grace, in what I refer to as Grace-Saturated Relationships, who will stand by us, believe in us, and never, ever see us as the problem but as precious people struggling with the problem.

Seek to Cooperate Less

It would be helpful if parents spoke to their children about problems and how they can invite them to cooperate with them instead of cooperating with things that would give them more of a fulfilling life. Whenever I have opportunity to speak with parents about healthy parenting practices, I encourage them to help their children make choices that are wise and to be patient as their children move from *what mom and dad said for me to do* to *what's the best choice* for them and others. Unfortunately, for a number of us we've not learned that problems tempt us to cooperate with them and each time that we do, it is easier and easier to keep cooperating.

As we reach adulthood we can encounter real difficulty "breaking up" with problems if we've been "going steady" with them for some time now. I've used the word picture of someone riding their bicycle from their house to the barn some 50 yards away. If they take the exact same path to and from the barn over a long period of time, after a while they will not even need to steer the bicycle since its wheels will be in a groove. However, if they choose to take another route, they will need to be intentional in steering until this is the new "groove." Choosing not to cooperate with problems is like forging a new path and this takes real work and attention, but we can do it.

Journey of Grace

Remember that life is more of a marathon run than a sprint and that God's grace is immeasurably more deep and rich than we could ever imagine. Be patient with yourself and yet persistent in dealing with problems—this is a journey of grace. Grace-Saturated People know this and respond accordingly. Life is a series of successes, failures, and all kinds of things in between. This comes as no surprise and there is never any shame doled out by Grace-Saturated People nor should there be any given by any of us to ourselves.

The journey of grace is possible as we come to understand and apply the realities of God's amazing grace to our everyday living.

5

Living the Grace-Saturated Life

FOR US TO EXPERIENCE healing in the depths of our souls we need to allow God access to these deep regions of our hearts. As noted earlier, our hearts are the containers of memories and the subsequent stories we have developed about these events. It is also the place where these memories continue to need healing to experience the abundant life God desires for us. But to invite God into these deep regions and the woundedness that resides there can be a rather intimidating experience unless we feel that we can fully trust God with what is found. But how else will we experience true healing without letting the Great Physician see us as we really are?

A number of us are much more comfortable with God's saving grace than with embracing grace for the many layers of our lives needing healing. Why? There are a number of obstacles that need to be overcome.

Fear Not

Fear is a big obstacle. Some have a deep, yet unstated, fear of God's reaction to us if we were to stand before the Holy One with our lives wide open. It is as if we trust in salvation while at the same time fearing what might be done if we *really* let God see deep inside of us. As someone once said, "Fear is the dark room where negatives are developed." When we fear God we believe something bad is sure to happen if we're honest about ourselves.

God knows that we struggle with fear. Fear of the unknown, fear of change, fear of punishment, fear of abandonment, and even fear of being who we are. Is it any wonder that the first words out of the angels' mouths when meeting with the shepherds were "fear not"? They had to settle the shepherd's fears before they would be able to hear the rest of their message about the birth of the Savior. We need to overcome fear to hear the good news of how approachable God is for those who are hurting.

God Loves Me but Does God Like Me?

When fear dominates our hearts, we have yet to experience the internal embrace of God's love. "Such love has no fear, because perfect love expels all fear. If we are afraid, it is for fear of punishment, and this shows that we have not fully experienced his perfect love" (1 John 4:18 NLT). Our experiences with others whose love is of the conditional variety can become the lens through which we view God's love. Assuming divine love for us is based upon our performance rather than God's character is dangerous ground to be on. I wonder how many of us really realize that love is the only characteristic definitive of God for Scripture shows us clearly that "God is love" (see 1 John 4:8).

> *A Moment for Reflection.* While on the topic of God's love I encourage you to read 1 Corinthians 13:4-8. This is commonly referred to as the "love chapter" as it lists the attributes of love that we are to live out with others. Too often when these verses are read we focus on ourselves to see how well we're doing. If, indeed, "God is love" (1 John 4:8) then we can read these verses in a new way. I suggest you begin each sentence with "God loves me and is . . . with me" so that the first part of verse 4 reads "God loves me and is *patient* with me" and the latter part as "God loves me and is *kind* with me." Wait until you reach verse 5 where it reads, "God loves me and *is not easily angered* at me and *keeps no records of wrongs.*"

Some of us can accept that God loves us but when asked if we believe we are *liked*, many would probably give pause before answering. This is due to the fact that we often experience a disconnect between these two terms in our everyday lives. How many times have we heard "I have to *love* them but I don't have to *like* them" as if to say our actions and commitment to treating others well constitutes "love" but our feelings about them relates to whether we "like" them or not. God does not make this distinction however. We are loved *and* liked because, once again, it is not about what we have and have not done; it is because of who God is and the great heart of the One who has created us.

Let's take a brief trip back to the creation story. The first two chapters of the very first book in our Bibles describe how God created all that exists, including us. Just prior to the creation of people, God reflected upon what was created so far and "saw that it was *good*" (Genesis 1:25). After creating human beings God "saw all that He had made, and it was *very good*" (1:31). I'd say that God liked what was created and *really liked* the creation of people even though fully aware that within a brief amount of time both the first man and first woman would make a decision that introduced pain and suffering. There were consequences from their decision but we do not see anywhere that God had a change of mind or heart toward them. To the contrary, Scripture shows us clearly that God had a plan for redemption in place *before* the creation of the human beings who made a decision to sin (see 1 Peter 1:18-21).

In short, we may feel much more able to profess faith in God as Savior and Lord of our lives while at the same time stopping short of professing the goodness and faithfulness of God to us evidenced in an unfailing love. This, too, is an area of growth and healing for us as it involves our views of God.

Broken Trust

Related to fear is the obstacle of trust. Often we have experienced a breach of trust in our relationships that has hurt us deeply. Possibly we have shared our struggle with a trusted other only to discover they broke silence and shared with someone else. Broken trust wounded us further and created in us an approach where we feel safest near the surface. If this is true with people, how much more true can it be with our relationship with God?

In an old story of a person who slipped and fell off a cliff, falling headlong toward certain disaster, they managed to grab hold of a ledge and held on for dear life. Shouting for help to anyone who could hear, a voice from above answered. "Let go of your grip," the voice said. Puzzled, the person shouted back, "Who are you?" "I'm God," said the voice, "Let go of the ledge and trust me." The person's next response is one that many of us can relate to. "Is there anyone else up there?!" Do I trust God enough to let go of my fear and land safely in loving hands as it relates to the struggles and sins we face day in and day out?

Shame

Another obstacle is shame. Shame has to do with our embarrassed feelings about having failed in some area of our lives. It is the discomfort that accompanies our disbelief at what we've done. Some people mistake feelings of shame with those of guilt. Guilty feelings are connected with having done something wrong whereas shameful feelings are related to there being something wrong with us as a result of doing something wrong. Can I share a little secret? We have ALL done things that we are not proud of. Scripture speaks of "all have sinned and fall short of God's glory" and until we embrace this humbly, we will feel that our sin is worse than others' sins. Shame can prevent us from laying open our hearts to God for fear that the divine reaction will be to induce shame.

Children of God

A final obstacle that must be overcome so that we can experience the embracing grace of God is the misunderstanding of what it means to be a child of God. I'm embarrassed to say how long it took me to really understand what it means to be a child of God. There are a number of reasons for this but I suspect one of the biggest ones is the set of beliefs that I developed while growing up in a church group that believed one could "lose their salvation" or "backslide." I recall being so afraid of losing my salvation that whenever an "altar call" was given, I would go forward to be prayed for to receive salvation *even after I had made a profession of faith on a number of occasions!* Thankfully one of those who came to pray for me noticed that this was an ongoing experience and assured me that I had made a commitment already and did not need to make one every time the opportunity was given.

It is my suspicion that others have had similar experiences to mine where the theological issue was not eternal security but rather *eternal insecurity.* Misunderstanding how salvation makes us children of God can get in the way of us drawing near and sharing our pain with our loving Lord. My early beliefs equated personal failures with the chance of rejection from God's family and were reinforced with some pretty fine examples of "fire and brimstone" sermons. It is not just theological beliefs that promote this fear that God will reject and eternally punish his children but also experiences with people whose acceptance was based upon some set of inclusion/exclusion criteria.

Ever notice that one of the first tasks in beginning to attend a new church is to discover what the "conditions of acceptance" are? I recall moving from one part of the country to another and had to find out what the "local sins" of the new church were. "Local sins" refers not so much to specific sins listed in Scripture but rather to actions and activities that fall into the realm deemed "matters of conscience." Examples abound but the common denominator is the invisible line that, once crossed, lands one outside the acceptance of others. If you've ever had this experience you know how important it is to find out the conditions of acceptance so that you don't experience any form of rejection.

God operates very differently than we do in this area. When we accept his very rich and gracious salvation, we are adopted into the family of God. We're not employees who can be fired and removed from the workplace for messing up; we are family members who, though imperfect, are still family. God the Father disciplines us for our good when we are out of alignment with family values, but never punishes his children by rejection or severely dealing with them.

Possibly you do not worry about being rejected from God's family but the issue of discipline strikes a nerve. Some of the woundings that we receive in life are unfortunately at the hands of family members—including parents. The word "discipline" creates fear for some who have received severe punishment and a tendency to hide from the one dishing it out.

To live the grace-saturated life we need to grow in our understanding of God and overcome any obstacles in the way. Only then will we see God as more grace-saturated than any of us could ever dream of being. In fact, the first step in living a grace-saturated life is to take steps in the direction of healing our concepts of God.

Conceptualizations of God

What are we talking about when we speak of a person's God concept? The term "God concept" generally refers to an individual's private or personal view of God. In other words, we all have an idea of what God is like and how God feels and behaves toward us. It is from this viewpoint that we conduct our lives. And because we do not know much about what God is actually like, we rely upon our perceptions (or conceptualizations) of who God is. We don't necessarily just interact with God *as God is* but rather how *we believe God to be.* Our concepts of God, then, are mental representations of perceived realities. So does that mean that we are not really dealing with God in our everyday lives? No, not at all. What it does mean, however, is that some of our preconceived notions of God can get in the way of us truly experiencing our God as loving and gracious towards us.

Let's take an example from our own lives. Let's say that before you and I ever met that you had heard certain things about me that are not true. For sake of example, let's say that you had heard from others that I am stern, cold, and distant in my interactions with others. Let's add that you had also heard from people you trust that I am a very busy person who gets irritated when people interrupt my schedule. If you believed these things to be true, how would you interact with me when we did meet? Would you conduct yourself a certain way? Would you even want to meet me since, from what you've heard, I'm not really the sort of person that you'd like to know. After all, what is wrong with me to conduct myself in such a way with people who simply want to meet me? The reality is that I've never been described in any of the ways just noted and enjoy interacting with others so much that "interruptions" of my schedule to talk with people are what I look forward to! But if you *believed these things to be true*, they would indeed flavor your view of me and any interactions that we might have.

Lessons Taught and Caught

Our ways of viewing God also are affected by what we have experienced in life and what we have learned in lessons *taught* (more formal training from Scripture such as one would receive in Christian education and what parents specifically teach at home about God) and *caught* (things we pick up from others in conversations about God, what others say God does and does not do, etc.). Although discussing the God concept could fill an entire book, let me say briefly how we develop our "perceived realities" about God.

Early interactions with parents and other caregivers sets the stage for seeing God a certain way. If we are adequately cared for and responded to when having needs such as hunger, affection, protection, etc., then we develop secure attachments. Having secure attachments creates an inner sense of security that the world around us is a safe place. If, however, we do not have such a positive environment then we have the sense of insecurity in the safety of this world and the relationships with those who could provide what we are wanting and needing. These early experiences then become the first strokes of the brush on the canvas of our internal worlds as we are coming to "paint" God's portrait on our hearts.

We continue to construct our views of God with other experiences and teachings that occur in interactions with others as we grow up. From this collection of early experiences and those that follow, we are developing a story about God that we then treat as if it is truly who God is. This would be fine if all of what we have collected is accurate, but that is not the case.

Adding to this, what happens in our larger circles of relationships affects our concepts of God. Those lessons *taught* and *caught* in our religious training or lack thereof, our relationships with people who profess a faith in God, and even from our experiences in life such as traumatic events and the meanings we make of these events as they involve what God should or should not have made/allowed to happen.

Context Counts

Jones pointed out an even broader sphere of influence in that "Concepts of God, nonetheless, are dyed deeply by the historical, geographical, social, and cultural environment." In brief, we do not develop our ideas about God within a vacuum. As I noted earlier, my formative years in the church culture I was exposed to factored into my God concept. I also grew up in a predominately blue collar, middle class, white family that I suspect was more Republican than Democrat even though we didn't talk much about politics. I'm a Michigander by birth and grew up in the Grand Rapids area. I'm a "middle kid" who believes things should be "fair." I'm also male and now in my early 50's. Did I mention that I'm an American? Maybe that goes without saying but I need to say living in America is different than other parts of the world. Is all of this important to the development of the God concept? Absolutely! These are all descriptions of the "seed bed" of my beliefs about God.

When I Was a Child

Phillips spoke to the developmental aspect of God concept development by writing, "The trouble with many people today is that they have not found a God big enough for modern needs." He continued, "While their experience of life has grown in a score of directions . . . their ideas of God have remained largely static." I'm reminded of the teaching contained in

1 Corinthians 13:11, "When I was a child, I talked like a child, I thought like a child, I reasoned like a child. When I became a man, I put childish ways behind me." This verse seems to point out the ideal. The reality, for a number of people, is that this is more a hope than present truth as it applied to the God concept. The reason for this is that we may continue to believe that God is a certain way well into our adult lives. Time passing may help us mature physically without much effort on our parts, but beliefs about God simply become more entrenched if not subjected to the editing power of the Spirit of God.

Philip Yancey gives a personal example of this in his book, *Reaching for the Invisible God*:

> As I consider my own assumptions about relating to God, I now see them as misguided and simplistic. From childhood I inherited an image of God as a stern teacher passing out grades. I had the same goal as everyone else: to get a perfect score and earn the teacher's approval. Cut up in class and you'll be sent to the back of the room to stand in the corner or to a vacant room down the hall. Almost everything about that analogy, I have learned, contradicts the Bible and distorts the relationship. In the first place, God's approval depends not on my 'good conduct' but on God's grace. I could never earn grades high enough to pass a teacher's perfect standards—and, thankfully, I do not have to. In addition, a relationship with God does not switch on or off depending on my behavior. God does not send me to a vacant room down the hall when I disobey him. Quite the opposite. The times when I feel most estranged from God can bring on a sense of desperation, which presents a new starting point for grace. Sulking in a cave in flight from God, Elijah heard a gentle whisper that brought comfort, not a scolding. Jonah tried his best to run from God and failed. And it was at Peter's lowest point that Jesus lovingly restored him.

> *A Moment for Reflection.* I would encourage you to take a few moments to reflect upon who you see God to be to you today. How would you describe him? What are his expectations of you? How have you come to see God this way? (i.e., where are the connections?) For example, you might find that you see God as only marginally patient and forgiving of your failings, expecting you to "get it right" in some area of your life or feeling like there is something "wrong" with you. Once you identify some of these beliefs and have spent a little time reflecting on where you came up with such beliefs, you might find that one or both parents held high expectations of you and that you didn't feel like you had much room for error. You might also have discovered that other people reinforced this idea by teaching things such as "good boys and girls . . . " which led you to believe yourself to be acceptable and good when being "good" and punished after having been "bad." It is important to realize that not everything deemed good or bad by others was truly good or bad behavior. For example, "being quiet while your father sleeps" might have been *preferred* of young children but was not necessarily *good* or *bad*.

Show Us the Father

At this point some readers might say, "Well, my view of God is what I have gained from the Bible." That is partially true for most of us but with a bit of a twist. Which part or parts of the Bible are we referring to? There are a number of ways that God is described throughout Scripture that provide partial views that may not portray him fully and in context. The disciples grappled with this very thing when we finally hear Philip speak up and ask Jesus to show them the Father that he spoke so intimately of on so many occasions. Jesus answered him in John 14:9 by saying, "Don't you know me, Philip, even after I have been among you such a long time? Anyone who has seen me *has seen the Father*" (emphasis added). Jesus helped the original disciples and those of us who follow him now to see that any conceptualization of God that is accurate *is one that is congruent with who Jesus is.* You may need to sit with that last sentence for a bit to really *hear* what it is saying.

In my counseling practice with a number of Christians over the years, many of their conceptualizations of God were far less than grace-saturated. In fact, one of the ways that Satan keeps us from finding healing in our lives is by working to distort how we view God. If he is successful in doing so, we will forever ask God from a distance to heal us without risking to come near for fear of finding God to be angry, impatient, or anything else that is less than grace-filled. Satan knows full well that a painfully distorted view of God will keep any number of us away from getting too close to him. Again, if Satan cannot destroy us, he will settle for a close second in that we are fearful of the One who loves us so very much and therefore continue to cover over our wounded hearts.

If, indeed, we can wrap our minds and hearts around the truth of what Jesus said, it will be so liberating! Imagine in your mind's eye that we come to Jesus with our hearts full of pain and confusion and find that he embraces us with all of our "stuff" and brings the warmth of his grace to bear upon these wounds. What comes to mind is a small child who has fallen and scraped their knee. When they come to Jesus with such wounds and the tears that so naturally follow, they find that he, like a loving parent, tenderly comforts the child while cleansing and gently kissing the painful wound. Can you envision such a gentle Healer coming to you in this way?

Layers of Life

Clearing up our God concept so that we can feel safe enough to approach God with all of our "stuff" sets the stage for us to find deeper levels of healing as we work through the various layers needing God's grace. Knowing that God is not only on our side in this healing process but also fully aware of what we will yet discover deep inside helps us to forge ahead without fear of judgment or shame. It is as if we have layers of life needing healing that can only be accessed as the outer ones find gracious healing first. It reminds me of how in my clinical work clients come in with what is called a "presenting concern" they desire help with, only to find that in some cases this problem is a much safer issue to address than what may lie beneath. How I manage the "presenting concern" sets the stage for deeper issues to be surface. If I were to respond with shock over the issue that is first presented, clients would not feel safe sharing anything that *really* concerns them. When I respond in a way that deepens trust in me as a counselor who can manage whatever wounds the person may carry, it allows deeper exploration of these areas and provides opportunity for insight and healing.

When we feel safe to be honest with ourselves and God about what is in the depths of our hearts, we can get at the root of problems that have plagued us for a good part of our lives. How else could it be that we would find healing at the deepest level if we never feel safe enough to go into those darker parts of our hearts? But when we find it safe to be who we are before

God, warts and all, then we can find what we so desperately need: deep healing as opposed to surface change.

Grace for Daily Living

Many people have a misperception of how life works as it applies to the problems we face. It seems that our problems can end up defining who we are and how we view ourselves rather than being seen as the struggles we deal with day in and day out. Recall again the problem of alcoholism as an example. Do we say that "Sue is a precious person who struggles with alcoholism" or do we say that "Sue *is* an alcoholic"? How about this one: do we describe Bill as "a child of God who seriously struggles with pornography" or as a "pornography *addict*"? When our problems take over our lives to the point where we no longer see ourselves as *people struggling with the problem* but rather as *people who are the problem*, we develop what might be called problem-saturated lives.

Have you ever gotten absolutely drenched in a rainstorm? If so, you know what it feels like to be wearing clothes that are saturated with water. They are heavy, often uncomfortably cold, and drape off our bodies in rather unattractive ways. This can somewhat paint the picture of what a problem-saturated life can look like. We find ourselves soaked in the problems of life and their consequences to the point that we walk around with a heavy burden that leaves us feeling cold while living in ways that do not really portray the beauty God had originally designed for our lives. And to top it off, we often make ourselves crazier still by thinking that unless we reach a state of relative or complete "rain-lessness" there is something wrong with us.

Isn't it peculiar how we can get duped into thinking that in this life we can reach a state where we will no longer struggle with the temptations and problems we find ourselves vulnerable to? It is as if we have come to believe what our pragmatic culture suggests over what the reality of Scripture portrays. Our culture says that if our faith is genuine, then that will be validated by a life of success over problems and sin; if this isn't the case, then the culture of pragmatism says our faith has some kind of flaw to it (pragmatism here being boiled down to the belief that if something *works* then it's worth holding onto, otherwise *it's no good*). This sets us up to be people who cannot really be honest about the struggles we encounter. This is especially true for a number of people in my counseling practice whose profession is pastoral ministry. We as a society often expect these individuals to live on lofty pedestals that they quickly come to find are impossible to live on for any length of time. We were not meant to live on pedestals; we were meant to live by grace each day.

Thorns in the Flesh

Let's look for a moment at the life of the apostle Paul and something he learned by experience. In one passage of Scripture he spoke of his "thorn in the flesh" which was seen as an affliction brought on by Satan. He prayed on several occasions God would take it away from him but noted it was not taken away. The account goes on to say that God's answer to Paul's situation was that his "grace was sufficient" for him on a daily basis. I am so glad the "thorn" was never defined or identified because it gives us a principle to apply to *all* of our afflictions from the enemy of our souls, Satan. Sure, we have a number of hypotheses about what Paul's thorn was but no one really knows—we just know it was a problem Paul struggled with. It was seen as coming from Satan, Paul was never totally delivered from it that we know of, and he relied upon God's grace to deal with it day after day. Think about this for a moment—what if Paul's problem was the same one that you are dealing with today? Would that make a difference in how you see things? How you see yourself? How you rely upon God's grace and mercy? What if Paul discovered something that his example can teach us today—that no matter what the problem is, it will only define us to the level we allow it to and that we must embrace the grace of Christ to find the necessary strength to face each day.

A Journey to be Taken

You see, many people think that life is a problem to be solved rather than a journey to be taken by God's grace. If we think solving all of our problems is the prerequisite to living a life that pleases God, then we are not yet learning from Paul's example. Paul lived a life wherein God's grace empowered him to deal with the "thorn" rather than the "thorn" defining his life in Christ. Could we say that Paul was a "dear saint of God who struggled with a thorn in the flesh daily" or would we define him as a "thorn addict" or "thornaholic"?

What parent on a trip with small children has not heard the almost universal words, "Are we there yet?" We laugh about it because it's such a common experience. A child's sense of time just doesn't quite match the reality of the many miles that have to be traveled before arriving at some distant location. And it seems that the more important the destination to the child, say, Disneyland or some other amusement park, the more intense and frequent the question is asked. Again, children have a different view of things and so asking how soon we'll arrive seems so natural, even if it is the 65th time in less miles than that! They are simultaneously excited to arrive and somewhat growing in their impatience at the time it takes to get there. Children aren't the only ones who become impatient on trips.

This journey we're on called "life" is one wherein a number of us are asking, "*Why* aren't we there yet?" as it applies to our growth in Christ. We read Bible passages that tell us the old has gone and the new has come; but we know the old has not totally gone and therefore the new seems to be a few more miles down the road. Other passages speak of putting off the old self and putting on the new. Yet we find that we have not fully put off the old ways of living nor have we arrived at the destination of the new self either. Oh yes, we may have assurance of being a Christian but we wonder why what we profess doesn't necessarily match how we live—at least not with the regularity we desire. Adding to the difficulty are the convoy of other people in our lives who are making the same trip yet from our vantage point are closer to the destination, or maybe farther away from it, than us? "Are we there yet?" seems to turn into an inner frustration of "No I'm not, but I think I *should* be." This creates a sense of there being something wrong with us that we don't dare share with others for fear they might reinforce our fears. So one option we often take is to hide our struggles. In other words, we protect ourselves by hiding from others our true condition. It seems that we revert to the same approach the first couple, Adam and Eve, took when they gave in to temptation—they covered up and hid from God who, up to that point, had met with them on a regular basis. We, too, become masters at camouflaging our faults to the point that we seem to develop dual lives—the one others see and the one we live. This is not only bewildering and frustrating to us, it also causes us to live incongruently in our everyday lives. We live one thing while professing it is possible to be something else. This approach creates an inner tension and leaves us longing to live a different life consistently while also becoming vulnerable to the latest popular formula for "getting it right."

Addiction and Grace

Another approach we might take is to reach out to others who haven't "arrived" yet either, people who are willing to admit that the journey is a long one and that we need each other in order to make it to our destination. In a recorded lecture given by M. Scott Peck on spirituality and addictions, I recall some things that really stood out to me. One of these was his assertion that he felt people struggling with addictions were the most spiritual people he had ever met. As he talked further, it made perfect sense as he said that these individuals get up in the morning with a prayer of need and desperation for God's intervention in their lives whereas people not struggling with addictions, don't have that same sense of urgency to their prayers. In other words, there is a big difference between the person who prays, "God, if you don't help me today, I will surely fail" and the one who simply asks for God's help in the day. Jesus once said that those who have been forgiven much love much and the same principle applies here. Those of us who recognize our great need for God's grace each day will surely find it versus those of among us who may feel very little need to embrace the grace of Christ for this day. I agree also with Mark McMinn's view that until we fully understand the depth of our sin condition, we will never fully appreciate God's grace.

Successful Churches

Something else Peck said caught my attention, namely that in his opinion, Alcoholics Anonymous (AA) was the most successful church in America. Having served in pastoral ministry myself, I had to listen further to see what it was about AA that was behind his statement. He continued by asking a question that went along these lines: How many churches do you know where you can stand up on a Sunday and say something like, "Hi, my name is David. It's been 6 days since I gave into _____" and have the congregation say, "Welcome David!" and even applaud my 6-day stretch of living above whatever the problem was. People in these groups have an understanding of the daily struggles we face and the tremendous power of grace needed for each new day.

Some might ask, "But shouldn't we strive to put off the old self behaviors and attitudes of the mind?" Yes! But I quickly add that it is an ongoing process with progress and set-backs all being a part of the journey. Jesus pointed out that the sick need a doctor and that He is the Great

Physician. He also is referred to as our Great High Priest who makes intercession for us as we struggle.

Take a moment and think about what kind of compassionate care and treatment a Great Physician and Great High Priest would have toward those they are serving. Are they impatient or condemning of those who come to them? I don't believe that could ever be the case. In fact, if you really want to know how approachable Jesus is, do a quick read through Scriptures to see who were most and least comfortable around him. What you'll find is that those who honestly admitted they struggled in life were met with great compassion whereas those who acted as if they had "arrived" were met with his greatest criticism.

Denial and Pride

You see, a common problem of people who cover over their problems is really a dual difficulty: denial, and the subsequent self-deception that travels with it, and pride. Denial is a defense we use against inordinate amounts of tension caused by the rift between what "is" and what "is supposed to be." A quick example is what some people do with their anger. If one believes it is wrong to be angry, which is a rather common misinterpretation of a few key Scripture passages by the way, then when angry feelings arise, they call it something else so as not to become angry. When someone cuts me off on the highway and I sense an unpleasant feeling welling up within me that is accompanied by less than godly thoughts, I am faced with admitting I am becoming angry. But if that is not an acceptable thing to me, I may say something like, "I'm not angry, I'm 'frosted!'" or "I don't get angry, I become 'burdened' though about some things." See how that works? If I don't call it what it is, I'm not really responsible for it—and I never really overcome it since I am not really dealing with it. A side effect of such an approach is that it easily turns into pride and arrogance so that what I don't like about myself *I can't stand in others!*

Judgment and Grace

The religious leaders of Jesus' day seemed to fall into such a camp and that was what really got to Jesus. He knew their hearts far better than they themselves did and saw how their denial of their own sin and struggles had developed into some rather grace-less living. So much so that we find examples such as the woman caught in the act of adultery being brought to him not for help and healing, but rather to force Jesus into a dilemma where he would either side with them and deliver judgment or be seen as someone who was soft on sin and therefore could not really be trusted for being spiritually on-track. Jesus responded with both judgment and grace in that scenario but it wasn't what the religious leaders were expecting. His judgment was upon the pride and arrogance behind the religious leaders' approach to this woman and his grace was extended to the woman who had become involved in an adulterous relationship. Isn't it interesting too that in that scenario Jesus stated that the one without sin would be the only one qualified to throw the first stone of judgment at the woman and yet, since he was the only qualified person there because of his sinless life, he chose to shower her with grace rather than stones. Talk about amazing grace!

The Worst Sinner is Not You!

The previous story involving the religious leaders of Jesus' day sheds some light on something else the Apostle Paul wrote about himself. In 1 Timothy 1:16 he shared his immense gratitude for God's grace being extended to him as the "worst" of all sinners and our quick read of this would have us equating his "worst sinner" status with the persecution of the church as his reason for claiming such a status.

Although Paul's behaviors were truly sinful toward other people, it leaves us wondering if he really *was* the worst of all sinners. After all, if we turn over to Philippians Chapter 3 we find that Paul had lived a pretty rigorous religious life to the point where he could even say of himself that he "obeyed the law without fault" (verse 6). Who among us can say that? In fact, if we're honest most of us would not be able to make such a claim.

Some reading these words would probably say, "Paul, you don't even want to hear all that I've done in this life." So Paul's words have often left me thinking that he was so thankful for God's grace he likely was exaggerating the importance of his failings in this passage. It seems that he was pointing out something bigger than the behavioral manifestations of sinfulness to what was underneath these actions. And maybe, just maybe, Philippians 3 gives us a clue. Could it be that when Paul shared all he at one time believed made him righteous that he was pointing out to us that he, being faultless in regard to religious right standing with God, was truly the worst of all sinners because he, more than anyone else, *had it together religiously to the point that he felt he had earned righteousness?*

We could say that among those religious leaders Jesus dealt with, Paul would have been leagues beyond them in his gracelessness while still thinking he *had it right with God.* When we are living by religious righteousness rather than by God's grace, it would seem sinful behaviors such as persecutions and injustices to others are the logical outcome. Paul had it so "right" that he indeed had become the worst of all sinners. It begs us to ask ourselves the question, "How are we seeking to be right with God?" Are we trying to "get it right" enough for God or do we really see our condition as one desperately needing his grace?

Grace-Saturated Living

We need to see our sin condition as it really is to fully embrace a grace-saturated life wherein we readily offer grace to others and to ourselves. We also need to be aware that usually our biggest obstacle to embracing God's grace is a misunderstanding of the process involved with change. With the example cited above, the absence of follow-up information might lead some to think that the woman charged with adultery instantaneously left her problems behind when Jesus told her to go and sin no more. That may have been the case but my suspicion, knowing how change occurs, is that it probably was a process rather than an event. Either way, it was by God's grace that this individual found help in making the life changes necessary to fulfilling her full potential in Christ.

When we do not understand how God works in and with us to affect change, we can also make our struggle worse by assuming he sees us the same way we see us—failures who cannot seem to overcome sinful choices. We may assume, and sometimes we have others assuming and proclaiming the same thing, that change should have happened by now in our walk with Christ. It's what I call the "six-month warranty on grace" approach that some seem to promote. It goes like this. We commit our lives to Christ and are welcomed *just as we are* into fellowship with other Christians since we know that not *everything* always changes at the moment of conversion, although we had hoped so! People know that it takes a while to make changes in one's life but how long, exactly, should that take? Three weeks? Maybe. Two months? Possibly. Beyond six months? Hmm, what's going on some might wonder.

Grace-Saturated People know that it is by God's grace we are saved *and* that we make changes over time—however long that is. In the second chapter of the book of Titus there is an interesting word that we need to pay attention to. "For the grace of God that brings salvation has appeared to all men. It *teaches* us to say 'No' to ungodliness and worldly passions, and to live self-controlled, upright and godly lives in this present age, while we wait for the blessed hope—the glorious appearing of our great God and Savior, Jesus Christ . . . ." (Titus 2:11-13, NIV; emphasis added). The word "teaches" says to me that we are not only saved by grace but also this very same grace leads us toward living in accordance with the new position we have in Christ. It is a process of change that God is more patient with than we ourselves.

Understanding Grace

Although what follows is by no means a treatise on grace, let me share a bit from Scripture to help us see more clearly how grace impacts our daily lives as we seek to become more like God in thought, word, and deed.

If we turn to the book of Ephesians we first see our need to establish a grace foundation upon which to build our lives.

> As for you, you were dead in your transgressions and sins, in which you used to live when you followed the ways of this world and of the ruler of the kingdom of the air, the spirit who is now at work in those who are disobedient. All of us also lived among them at one time, gratifying the cravings of our sinful nature and following its desires and thoughts. Like the rest, we were by nature objects of wrath. But because of his great love for us, God, who is rich in mercy, made us alive with Christ even when we were dead in transgressions—*it is by grace you have been saved.* And God raised us up with Christ and seated us with him in the heavenly realms in Christ Jesus, in order that in the coming ages *he might show the incomparable riches of his grace, expressed in his kindness to us in Christ Jesus. For it is by grace you have been saved, through faith— and this not from yourselves, it is the gift of God—not by works, so that no one can boast.* For we are *God's workmanship,* created in Christ Jesus *to do good works, which God prepared in advance for us to.* (Ephesians 2:1-10, NIV; emphasis added)

We see from this passage that out of God's great love for us who were so undeserving, the One who is rich in mercy made provision for our salvation through grace as verse 5 indicates, "It is by grace you have been saved." God did this to show how great and unmatched his grace is to us.

If there is any doubt as to our ability to change ourselves into being good enough to deserve God's favor, verse 8 reminds us that it isn't about anything we *have done, are doing,* or *will do someday* that brings such grace to us—it is all about the great gift of grace being given to us! What is our part in this then? We must receive it by faith. That's it. Period. And that, my friends, is often the rub as we tend to think that such a great gift should have a huge price tag. It indeed does, but we are not asked to pay for it since the only One would could afford such a cost, Jesus Christ, has already paid for it.

You'd think that would be explanation enough for us but I suspect that I am in good company when I say that I have not always lived like this is entirely true. I've tried and tried to *help* God not so much with the past sins in my life, but with overcoming the present and future ones. This misunderstanding on my part of what the grace of God was all about came about as a result of lessons *taught* and lessons *caught* from others in the Christian community. Yes, God's grace was good enough to cleanse all past sin but it was somehow up to me and him to "clean up my act" as it involved present and future living—and it wasn't happening at any rate that would set new ground speed records! The error in what I had learned is that it is an ongoing process of growth that takes time and a daily reliance upon God's marvelous grace.

Let's not leave this passage of Scripture too soon. Ephesians 2:10 speaks beyond our daily struggles to the purpose for our growth: " . . . so that we can do the good things He planned for us long ago" (NLT). What an amazing thought! It's not really about what we are doing to try to put off the old self to become more acceptable to God each day; we are already acceptable to him through this great gift of grace received by faith. We can now turn our attention away from trying to earn it to the bigger plan that God has for us—to live out the lives divinely planned for us long ago. To discover and live our Grace-Saturated Narratives.

We Are Not Home Yet

What about this everyday living of the Christian life? I mean, isn't there a time in life when the old self truly has gone and the new shows up fully . . . and stays? Well, as I was just pointing out, spiritual growth is a process and there is no real time frame on us "getting there" other than the fact that we all arrive once we leave this life and are made fully congruent with our position in Christ. At that time, the old self truly will be gone and we will have fully put on the new self. But we are not there yet.

In the meantime we must come to understand that as long as we're in this life we face a daily struggle of which kingdom values will most clearly be lived out this day, this hour, this very moment, for our lives are in a tug-o-war for our choices (as noted in the section on John 10:10). Galatians Chapter 5 reminds us, "These two forces are constantly fighting each other, and your choices are never free from this conflict . . . but . . . you are no longer subject to the law" (verses 16-18). What two forces? The Spirit and flesh.

Cooperating with the Spirit, Not the Flesh

"Wait a second," you might say, "didn't you earlier say that we can often confuse us with the problems that we struggle with?" Yes, I did. So how is it then that now there seems to be in Scripture an indication that we indeed are part of the problem (i.e., it is *my flesh*, me, that is prone to want to do its/my own thing that is contrary to God's plans)? Well, here is how I see it. When the first couple sinned by disobeying God, the entirety of creation was affected by that sin. This wonderful place called earth and all that live upon it were marred by this spiritual pandemic that can only be cured through the acceptance and application of Christ's redeeming life, death, and resurrection. This occurs in our lives by faith in him and his grace but is still "in the works" for this planet and all creation.

Even after we accept Christ's grace and enter into a new life in him we are still, however, battling each day to live in ways that are in line with his kingdom's values and plans. Remember the section from the Lord's Prayer where we ask that his kingdom come and his will be done on earth "as it is in heaven"? Or Paul's words regarding our daily decision to "die daily" to the desires that used to rule over us? Or Jesus' words to take up our crosses and follow him? What is being shown to us is that even though we are his children by our acceptance of his great gift of grace, we daily live with the lingering effect of sin that is manifested in a *proclivity toward*, or an *attraction to*, things contrary to his kingdom's values and principles. We have a *choice*, actually a series of choices, every day whether we will cooperate with the leading of the Spirit or with the drawing of sin's lingering effect upon this world. The first which leads toward maturity in our walk with Christ and the development of lives that more clearly portray God's kingdom whereas the other leads us into living in ways that hinder God's kingdom from being lived out fully through our lives.

Galatians 5:19 tells us that "When you follow" (or I might choose the word *cooperate*) "with the desires of your sinful nature . . . " and goes on to list what such choices produce. Later, in verse 25, it gives us the other side of the daily battle wherein it reads, "If we are living now by the Holy Spirit, let us follow" or again I would choose the words *cooperate with* "the Holy Spirit's leading in every part of our lives." In other words, when we are saved by God's grace we begin learning how to say "yes" to the leading of the Spirit in our lives and learn to say "no" to those things that would lead us away from all that God has in mind for our lives. This battle then is a battle over who and what I will *cooperate with* each and every moment of the day. In this life spiritual growth is evidenced by a higher percentage of cooperation with the Spirit than with those things that entice us to live in ways contrary to what God has in mind for our lives.

Winning Point

Take the sport of basketball for example. Most of us have been to a basketball game at some time in our lives or have watched one on television. My question is this: how do we determine the winner of the game? Simple answer: the one with the highest score when the game clock reaches zero. Let's take that a bit further. How many points does a team need to win by? Simple answer again: only one.

Okay, so the score does not have to be 100 to 0 for a win, it only needs to be 100 to 99 for a win. You may be sensing where I am going with this. Some people think that to have a "winning day" as a Christian, they must score 100 to 0 (or at least 100 to 10 or 20) or there is something wrong with them. I challenge that and say that a winning day is one where we score even one point more in our *cooperating* with the Spirit of God than with the former way of living. This fits better with where many of us live and can serve as a help in overcoming condemnation while at the same time encouraging us to find ways to "improve our game" so to speak.

Continuing with the metaphor of basketball a bit further, some of us need help in developing skills for offense such as shooting, passing, and working well with others. Others need to improve their defense such as keeping our guard up against the opponent's shots, paying attention to the areas needing to be covered, and keeping an eye on what our opponents are trying to set up. All of us need to work on our "conditioning" so as to be able to finish the game well. These can all be worked on but they take time and effort. And even with all the work that we do, we will still be "scored on" in the daily game of living because we have an active opponent (Satan) who seeks to have us cooperate with anything that goes against the kingdom of God. We also still carry with us the effect of the first couple's sin in that we have a proclivity toward cooperating still with those things that run contrary to God's ways and plans for our living.

The Book of James helps us better understand this daily battle with temptation where it notes, "Temptation comes from the lure of our own evil desires. These evil desires lead to evil actions, and evil actions lead to death" (1:14-15). "Evil desires" is another way of speaking of this *proclivity* toward sinning that is a lingering effect of sin's impact with which we live daily. When we cooperate with evil desire it leads us toward poor choices that, over time, usually lead us to an existence no longer filled with life but rather death on so many levels. Going back to the example of basketball, if we cooperate more and more with evil desire to the point that we're losing daily at a rate of 100 to 10 (or 5 or 1) then we are missing out on the "winning season records" God had in mind for us.

Let's leave the basketball metaphor for some real life examples to make this point more applicable. Let's say that one of the particular areas of struggle is how I view people and treat them as a result. Since God desires for health in our relationships, what if I continue to put myself first even though I am painfully aware I am both harming those around me and living a life of self-centeredness that will not bring God's kingdom to earth relationally. If I live in such a way I will find that my relationships will suffer to the point of having dead or, at least, less than healthy ones. I can choose to do so even as a Christian but that is so far removed from God's plans. Or let's say a particular area I am dealing with is my relationship with "stuff" (i.e., money, possessions, you know, "stuff"). I can continue to live in ways that accumulate all of these temporal things to the point I have truly "gained the whole world and lost my own soul." I would be choosing to cooperate with "evil desires" as opposed to cooperating with the Spirit's leading. The Spirit desires to guide me into a better and healthier way of living with each passing day.

Grace and Sin

The apostle Paul had obviously made it so clear to those he was speaking to regarding grace that some in the crowd must have started connecting the dots, but not in a good way! Paul showed how immense this grace of God is for help in daily living to the point that people around him must have thought, "Hmm, if grace is that great, then maybe it doesn't really matter how I live my life. In fact, it would seem that the greater my sin, the greater God's grace will be shown."

Paul's response showed he understood that people could take such grace in the wrong way but quickly noted how we can choose now to cooperate with the Spirit or continue cooperating with sin.

> Well then, since God's grace has set us free from the law, does that mean we can go on sinning? Of course not! *Don't you realize that you become the slave of whatever you choose to obey?* You can be a slave to sin, which leads to death, or *you can choose to obey God, which leads to righteous living. Thank God!* Once you were slaves of sin, but now you wholeheartedly obey this teaching we have given you. Now you are free from your slavery to sin, and you have become slaves to righteous living. Because of the weakness of your human nature, I am using the illustration of slavery to help you understand all this. Previously, you let yourselves be slaves to impurity and lawlessness, which led ever deeper into sin. *Now you must give yourselves to be slaves to righteous living so that you will become holy.* When you were slaves to sin, you were free from the obligation to do right. And what was the result? You are now ashamed of the things you used to do, things that end in eternal doom. But now you are free from the power of sin and have become slaves of God. *Now you do those things that lead to holiness and result in eternal life.* For the wages of sin is death, but the free gift of God is eternal life through Christ Jesus our Lord. (Romans 6:15-23 NLT, emphasis added)

You will notice Paul focused his attention more on those desiring to change than on those desiring to find some way of continuing to live in old ways that led to death.

Paul pointed out that we make choices now that lead to ever-deepening allegiance to sin or to God. His plea was for us to change our commitment from living for the disease of sin, that kills us on all levels, to living for God, which brings life on all levels. As we continue to choose to follow the life-giving ways of the Spirit we can experience the abundance of life of which John 10:10 speaks.

This is why Paul makes an impassioned case for giving our lives to God as a living sacrifice in Romans 12.

> And so, dear brothers and sisters, I plead with you to give your bodies to God because of all he has done for you. Let them be a living and holy sacrifice—the kind he will find acceptable. This is truly the way to worship him. Don't copy the behavior and customs of this world, but let God transform you into a new person by changing the way you think. Then you will learn to know God's will for you, which is good and pleasing and perfect. (Romans 12:1-2 NLT)

The path to transformation involves choosing daily to cooperate more and more with the Spirit's leading and less and less with the draw of evil desires. It is a learning process, as noted above, that we must realize doesn't take place overnight or even within 6 months, but rather a process of change that affects our thoughts and choices.

These changes in thought and choices affect our behavior and the end result is a life that is coming more and more into alignment with what God had in mind for us from the beginning. God sees us in our humanity and is daily providing the means for us to put off our old ways of living and put on his new ways. God's grace is so great and his power so strong that he will bring about the changes that we both God and we desire.

So What?

Once I heard someone say that when he prepared a message he always asked himself the question, "So what?" before he was done. If he couldn't make application, he went back and reworked the message until he could answer the question with some practical applications. The "so what" of this chapter on grace can be seen by discussing its impact upon three different, yet interrelated, relationships: with God, with self, and with others.

The first relationship this discussion impacts is with God. We must first and foremost understand that the idea of such rich and deep grace comes from our loving and merciful God. He knows the sin condition this world lives with and its lingering impact upon us better than anyone else ever could. He knows how the enemy of our souls seeks to have us cooperate with those things that harm us and in such deceitful ways as to have us thinking there is something terribly deficient with us. God's grace not only saves us, it also patiently teaches us to cooperate more with God's ways that lead us into the abundant life he desires for us. He also knows how the enemy of our souls lies to us about such a great gift of grace and so God clearly points out in his Word the truth about his grace. This is also one of the best ways we can understand how God truly sees our condition as opposed to how we think he sees us, which is often very negative and is usually based in distortions about God and his grace.

Having a better understanding of grace also impacts our relationship with ourselves. When we come to better appreciate the growth process and how God's grace works with us in it, we can offer much more merciful understanding to ourselves as we learn to follow God and his ways. Once we gain a better understanding of God's grace, we are situated to take on the next big barrier—our lack of grace to ourselves. You see, sometimes it is easier to see that God is forgiving and understanding while at the same time believing we should remain tough on ourselves.

Some of the reasons we are so grace-less to ourselves include some unhealthy views about discipline and punishment, often linked to our upbringing. We may believe on some deep level that all failings must be punished and since God's grace covers for the cosmic punishment, we somehow need to take care of it on a more "local" basis. And so we tend to beat ourselves up for failing *yet again* in whatever areas we struggle with so that after this self-abasement, we will have "paid for" such a failing.

Regarding this approach, I recall hearing someone say, "So, is Christ's sacrifice not good enough to pay for this sin to the point that one must do more?" The obvious answer is "No!" We need to learn how to fully accept Christ's sacrifice for sins and the wonderful grace he offers to the point that we can truly forgive ourselves.

A simple exercise may help. The next time you cooperate with evil desire in your life and confess that to God, stand in front of a mirror and say to yourself, "God's Word tells me that if I confess my sins to him, he will faithfully forgive me (see 1 John 1:9). Now, what more do I have to do above his sacrifice to have you forgive me?" You might be surprised to see how you have adopted extra conditions for forgiveness that even God may not have.

You might also add to this exercise a little truism that can help to dissolve distorted thinking regarding forgiveness. Try writing the following on a sticky note and placing it on the mirror: "Acceptance *does not equal* approval." When we fail to forgive ourselves and others, we are also often rejecting the person until they "get it together." Notice from the life of Christ, however, that he modeled acceptance of people whose lives were steeped in things he would not approve of but he loved them and reached out to them. Forgiving self and accepting self do not have to equate to approving of all that you have done. In fact, isn't forgiveness all about finding peace with things in your life, and the lives of others, that you do not approve of?

Everett Worthington wrote that there are two things necessary for us to forgive: empathy and humility. Empathy is the ability to "walk in another's shoes" so to speak. This isn't as difficult when we apply it to ourselves, for we indeed *are walking* in our own shoes. It seems to be more the second part that is the problem for us. You might quickly question that, since we are humbly confessing our sins to God when we fail. I'm not speaking something different. What I see happening when we fail to forgive ourselves is a disguised form of pride welling up at that moment that seems to be saying to us, "You're better than this. You shouldn't fail in this way any more or ever!"

For us to forgive ourselves and truly offer grace to the one living "in our shoes," we must fully embrace the truth that even though we desire to fully follow God, there is another force at work in us and around us that battles for our choices and "scores points" on us. When we truly come to understand that we can and do still cooperate with wrong choices in our thinking and living, we become better at offering grace and forgiveness to ourselves. Make no mistake, we do live with the consequences of our choices, good and bad, but we do not have to live with unrelenting guilt and condemnation from them.

Once we come to better understand God's grace and its application to our lives, we can be in much better position to offer it to others. We are all in this life situation together and need to learn to offer grace to others as we are learning to offer it to ourselves. When we reflect back upon the words of Jesus, who summed up fulfilling all the law and the prophets by loving God with all that we are and loving others *as ourselves*, we quickly see that we must learn to love. True love of self is evidenced in learning to forgive ourselves. Only as we learn to love and forgive ourselves can we appropriately love and offer forgiveness and grace to others.

This also works in reverse order at times as a starting point. I have known people who can readily forgive and offer grace to others yet really struggle to offer it to self. For some reason they have come to see themselves as undeserving of grace yet are able to see that others deserve it. Oftentimes this is a result of some really deep pain in the person's life that came in the form of shaming by powerful figures, possibly parents and/or graceless people. At other times it may be from deep wounding from others, possibly abuse of some form. In such situations, I have worked with people to learn to befriend themselves and offer the same grace that they would offer a friend. This is difficult work when abuse (verbal, physical, sexual, spiritual, or other forms) is involved and may necessitate working through it in the process of counseling to find inner healing.

The apostle Peter once asked Jesus how many times we are expected to forgive. When Jesus answered "seventy times seven" it was a way of saying "as many times as necessary." We need to expand upon the significance of what he was saying. Too often we look at this to apply it only to how many times I am to forgive others. That is too thin a reading of this principle. A richer reading would say that *in addition to* this verse applying to how many times I forgive and offer grace to others, we need to apply it to the one in the mirror. These verses tell us how many times we need to forgive and offer grace to ourselves as we walk with Christ in this life. Why? Because it is also the number of times that God forgives and offers grace to you and me on this journey. Innumerable!

Cooperating with the Spirit

For us to truly live out a grace-saturated life, we must clear up misconceptions of the God who desires to bring healing into the depths of our souls. To do so we need to examine how we have come to see God and make changes in these views as we compare and contrast these ideas with Who we see Jesus to be in Scripture. When we are able to do this, the Spirit of God can do some pretty remarkable healing within us. But we need to remember also that change is often a lengthy process and if God has a good plan and not a hurried one, why are we expecting change at a greater pace? The encouragement to "Throw off everything that hinders and the sin that so easily entangles" (Hebrews 12:2) is a call to cooperate more with the Spirit's leading. The result is that we attain more of what God intends for us. We are in the process of developing grace-saturated lives wherein we listen less readily to sin's voice and more quickly to promptings of the Spirit, keeping in step with the Spirit as a result. This involves a better understanding of how change occurs and the richness of grace for each day of life.

6

Grace-Saturated Relationships

EVEN THOUGH I AM not a medical researcher who has found a cure for cancer, I have found a remedy for what takes the life of many people around the world and leaves others existing but not really living. The biggest killer of human beings is not some disease of the body but rather a disease of the heart and soul created by a plethora of "thin" and/or wounding relationships and a dearth of what I call Grace-Saturated Relationships (GSRs).

Think about it for a second. Aren't we created for relationship from the time our mothers and fathers hold us in their arms when we enter this world to the day when we sit holding the hand of our loved ones as they close their eyes for the last time? We came into this world as relational beings and did everything we could to attach to those around us. We cooed, cuddled, and even cried out to be held. Can I let you in on a little secret? We haven't changed. We still need people and the relationships that they give us, but there is the catch.

Conditions of Acceptance Revisited

As newborn babies we have some "hard wired" strategies to help us survive and thrive. As any parent can tell you, there are different kinds of cries that children have that elicit different responses from caregivers. A "fussy" cry is responded to much differently than a "pain" cry. Researchers studying a village of people noticed the immediate response of adults to a cry of pain coming from a child. The adults ran to the location to help. The world we live in every day can be very different than such a village. Sometimes our cries of pain elicit the response of predators or the alienation of friends, or both!

As written in an earlier chapter, many relationships are marked by conditions of acceptance. Seeking to discover what I must do and not do, be and not be to be accepted is so wearying and invites us to live inauthentic lives. Endorsing and/or adhering to a "conditions of acceptance" approach to others invites rejection and offense. Rejection is experienced by those who don't quite measure up to the stated or tacitly assumed conditions. Offense is felt by those having experienced what someone once called the "right foot of fellowship." Rejection and offense are most definitely the by-products of a "conditions of acceptance" approach to relationships.

"Give Me a Bible, I'll Show Him!"

When I was a teen I became a follower of Christ. As you might imagine I wanted to associate with other teens who also were seeking to follow Christ and so one night at a pizza shop it happened. To set the stage a bit, it was the 1970s and I had hair much longer than I do now. If you saw the picture of me as a high school football player, you would understand why I can relate to the look of professional football players, such as Troy Polamalu of the Pittsburgh Steelers, whose hair noticeably flows out from their helmets.

There I sat with my friend "Grizz" enjoying a pizza, and the company of each other, and the attractive waitress who was serving us, when a group of about 8-10 teens came into the nearly deserted pizza shop. They looked squeaky clean so I glanced over a few times to see if there was anything else different about this group. Their pizza came and I saw them bow their heads and return thanks for the meal, a sure sign of some kind of allegiance to faith it seemed. I said to Grizz, "They're Christians too. I'm going to go say hello." To my surprise, Grizz said, "Don't do it." I asked, "Why?" but I don't think I listened to his response because I'd made up my mind that I wanted to connect with them.

Walking over to the table full of teens and I began, "Hi. I noticed you all prayed over your meal so you must be Christians. I am too." It seemed innocent enough so imagine my dismay when the guy I was standing behind turned and said, "You know it's a sin to have long hair, right?" There were many things I knew at that moment but this was not one of them. I replied, "Um, well, whatever . . . I just wanted to stop over and say hello and say it's great to see you unafraid to show your faith by giving thanks before eating." I thought I was safely exiting the scene with that statement and noticing my feet starting to walk back to my table, but then it came. "Someone give me a Bible, I'll show him."

Grizz is a good friend and so he didn't say "I told ya' so." We simply finished our meal and left. I made it all the way to the parking lot before I felt a surge of anger. Grizz, being four years older than me, understood more than I gave him credit for and was there to help calm me down. I still owe him for the crack my fist put in his dashboard but that's another story.

Movement Versus Institution

Were these bad kids at the pizza shop? Not really. In fact, they were probably very well behaved teens who had real zeal for what they believed and it seemed to serve them well. They knew what they believed and held tenaciously to it, sharing it with others who happened along. Oftentimes, however, what begins as a passion for knowing God can evolve into a set of rules that define the relationship.

Parker Palmer wrote about the difference between "movements" and "institutions" in his book *Courage to Teach*. He explained how movements are alive and full of energy and creativity. Movements aren't so much concerned about *what has been* but really flourish thinking about *what could be*. Institutions, on the other hand, are generally movements that have lost this zest for *what could be* and settled into survival mode. The energy of institutions is often channeled into ways to stay solvent.

Movements and institutions are all made up of people who entered them for some reason at some point in time. Movements are full of people willing to give of themselves for the cause they believe in; institutions need people willing to give of themselves but often have lost sight of the cause that brought them together. Sadly, I believe this is true of people of faith as well. The teens had no doubt experienced the grace of Christ at some point but by the time I met them were more focused on being "right" than on accepting someone very different than them.

Pharisees Don't Get Any Respect

The Pharisees, like the late Rodney Dangerfield, often "don't get any respect." I sometimes feel as bad for them as I do for Christians today. What!?

Yes, there seems to be a connection that I believe I can unpack before this book hits the floor.

In my graduate training in seminary I thought I would do a bit of research on these pesky fellows that we find harassing Jesus and his followers in the Gospels. What I found surprised me. The Pharisees of Jesus' day were a long shot from those who first made up this *movement*. Originally they were so zealous for God and pleasing him that they were considered the evangelists of their day. They so loved God that they wanted to share this with others. Their passion for God led them to spell out all the ways one could please or displease God. Their original intention was to do those things that were pleasing God while refraining from those that were displeasing.

If you can imagine such zeal being put into living a life for God it would epitomize the movement described by Palmer. But these are not the Pharisees we meet in the Gospels by and large. What we find is a group of people who were so focused on *getting it right* that they got it absolutely *wrong!* I've seen this cycle play out far too often where people who begin so well end up so far from where they began. In fact, people focused on *getting it right* more times than not end up *getting it so wrong*. They seem to have swapped life for law.

> *A Moment for Reflection.* Take a moment to think about where you are on the continuum of life on one end and law on the other. Are you more focused on *getting it right* than on experiencing and offering grace to others? How are you doing in your relationships with others? Are they strained as you or they are seeking to meet *conditions of acceptance*? How about the church in which you worship? Is there more emphasis on *getting it right* or *accepting people where they are for as long as they need to be there* because of their great worth as people? Are you a member of movement or an institution?

When we first experience God's saving grace we are changed people indeed. This gift that is so freely given to us motivates us to share it with others. Along the way, however, we can be tempted to focus more on *how to please God* than to continue enjoying and sharing this grace. This puts us in danger of becoming an institution like the Pharisees of Jesus' day rather than continuing to be people of this marvelous movement of grace.

Open My Heart, Heal My Soul

As I wrote in an earlier chapter, our hearts and souls get wounded in this life by a variety of hurts and disappointments. This world has become a dangerous place for many where the wounded feel a need to remain silent for fear of further hurt. Indeed, some people have been raised in homes and environments where the three rules of "dysfunctional" families remain intact: don't talk, don't feel, don't trust.

Some have been raised to believe they should never speak of the things they have experienced. The old adage that "children should be seen and not heard" takes on even more power when it applies to abuses being suffered. Not only does a person suffer from the abuse, they suffer silently as well.

Adding to the "gag order" is the second rule: don't feel. Children who have been taught to ignore their feelings often grow up to do the same in other relationships, thus perpetuating a lifestyle of incongruent emotional responses. For example, what would normally invite one to experience anger doesn't do the same in a person living by this rule. They indeed experience anger but, since it cannot be expressed, usually have to find someplace else to put it. Depression can be one of the places that unexpressed anger resides. Self-loathing can be another landing place for unexpressed negative emotion.

The third rule of not trusting others completes the three-walled prison cell many reside in. "Who would believe me anyway?" has been so reinforced over time that the person wouldn't dare share their hurt and pain with another. To find healing in the depths of our being, we must find a safe place, a safe person who will offer the grace needed for us to find deep healing.

Escaping from the prisons of our past requires relationships that are safe and full of genuine grace.

Grace-Saturated People Needed

Grace-Saturated Relationships (GSRs) require Grace-Saturated People (GSP) to create the conditions wherein people can feel safe enough to un-apologetically be themselves, tell their stories, and experience new ways of living life to its fullest. I'm convinced that it is nearly impossible to find the healing we need without having at least one person in our lives who is grace incarnate to us.

> *A Moment for Reflection*. Sit with the term "grace incarnate" for a moment. Grace embodied in human form or, better, a person whose very nature speaks grace to our woundedness. Think of the people you have felt most comfortable around, most accepted by. Have they not had the scent of grace about them?

In the Book of James we read, "Confess your sins to each other and pray for each other so that you may be healed" (5:16, NLT). What a wonderful verse that can too often be read too thinly. A rather thin reading only focuses on the accountability that fellow Christians can provide for one another. A deeper reading of this verse shows us the tremendous power for healing that is imbedded in a Grace-Saturated Relationship. To experience its richness we need to break it down a bit.

Confess is an act of telling. When I confess something, I tell the story of some aspects of my life. I throw off excuses, blaming, rationalization, and every other hiding behavior and with heart wide open I speak my life to another. But it is the confession of *my sins* that this verse says brings healing. "Yikes!" is the response of most of us for we do not know what the other will do with this information.

Missing the Mark

It is interesting to me how often people only have one understanding of the word "sin." Sure, the word has to do with our willful choosing of things that are contrary to God's best plans for our lives and often very harmful to us and others BUT that's not all there is to the story. It's helpful for us to understand "sin" as also being described as "missing the mark."

Though I am not really much of an archer, I owned a compound bow years ago, thinking I would become proficient in my practice and possibly go bow hunting but discovered quickly that it takes *lots* of practice to train oneself to hit what you're aiming at. Even with a compound bow I discovered muscles I must have never used before by the way they were aching. Needless to say, archery is something one has to work at to place an arrow in the bulls-eye. Living life is much like archery in that we have to spend quite a bit of time and energy working on becoming proficient at "hitting the mark."

Someone once said "Good choices are the product of wisdom; wisdom is the product of experience; and experience is the product of bad choices." We all have missed the mark and fallen short of God's best plans for us (see

Romans 3:23). Since this is a common experience, it would seem that there wouldn't be much fear involved with confessing we have missed the mark to others, but there is great fear for so many. Why? Because the "each other" that we are to share our history of failings with may or may not be grace-saturated.

Where Grace Meets Human Need

When we do, however, find someone that we can share the deep hurts, wounds, and failings with safely, we find where God's grace meets humanity. Think about this for a moment. The Bible tells us that where two or three are gathered in his name, Jesus is there (Matthew 18:20). Jesus was truly grace-incarnate when walking the face of the earth. Grace so flowed from his life that little children ran to him, "sinners" invited him over to their homes and parties, and religious folks were irritated by him. So, it's safe to say that where one follower of Christ who needs to share their heart of pain meets with another follower of Christ who is grace-saturated, they are joined by the One who was and is fully grace-incarnate. In this grace-saturated meeting of three we can experience healing!

Grace-Saturated People

George Eliot had an idea of what a Grace-Saturated Relationship was like: "Oh, the inexpressible comfort of feeling safe with a person; having neither to weigh thoughts nor measure words, but to pour them all out, just as they are, chaff and grain together, knowing that a faithful hand will take them and sift them, keep what is worth keeping, and then, with the breath of kindness, blow the rest away."

When we experience such a relationship we feel so safe that we can then explore areas of our lives that we don't even want to recall. Grace-Saturated Relationships need Grace-Saturated People. But what, exactly, does such a person *look like?*

Comfortable Presence

Grace-Saturated People are comfortable to be around. It would seem to go without saying that a telltale sign of a grace-saturated person is that we feel at ease when with them. I recall receiving one of the greatest compliments

I've ever received from a co-worker some years ago. In talking with the person one time over lunch he said, "You wear your Christianity more comfortably than anyone I know." As we talked further it was apparent to me that he was speaking of my presence when with him and others. A certain comfort was there in the moment that transcends any explanation other than grace was present.

Make no mistake though, being comfortable to be around does not always bode well with those who resent grace. Unfortunately there are a number of people who profess Christianity that seem to resent grace and, instead, favor rules and regulations. They so desperately focus their energies on "getting it right" that they inevitably get it wrong. They miss grace in a pursuit of the allure of perfection. This also sets grace-saturated people apart.

Give Up on the Myth of Perfection

Grace-Saturated People have given up on the notion of flawless perfection in themselves and others. I recall talking with a seasoned pastor one time about the reality of our human experience when he made a wise observation: "The Bride of Christ has never been clean . . . but she's still his bride." Another church leader shared with pastors a bit of wisdom when he said they would have less stress if they looked out on the congregations and could see them as more "carnal" (imperfect, choosing to do things that are less than what God would desire of them) than "spiritual" (nearly perfect). Why? Because that's how we are!

Hebrews 4:16 states, "So let us come boldly to the throne of our gracious God. There we will receive his mercy, and we will find grace to help us when we need it." (NLT). Our High Priest understands our situation and how we are still in need of his grace and mercy each day as we are growing more and more into his likeness in our daily living. If we had it right, we would not need a High Priest offering this for us.

> *A Moment for Reflection.* What is your visceral response to the idea that none of us have arrived at perfection yet? Admitting our condition is not synonymous to saying it's okay (remember, "acceptance is not equal to approval") but is necessary to develop a grace-saturated approach to life. *I need grace, you need grace, we all need grace . . . daily!* If your initial response was one of irritation or strong disagreement, I'd encourage you to delve deeper to see if something might be underneath a negative reaction to accepting the fact that we need more than saving grace; we need daily grace because we're daily in need of it, which means we're no where near *perfect.*

Walls of Protection

Grace-Saturated People are good at seeing through smoke screens and facades knowing they are but walls of protection. A dear friend of mine has a rather crusty exterior. From a distance you might wonder if he's safe to be around. He is tall, wears black leather, has wild flowing hair, and a loud voice. His tone is blustery and seems like it has a real "don't mess with me" edge to it. I love the guy! Why? Because I know the *real* person that he is. You see, my friend has one of the biggest, tender hearts you would ever want to encounter. He even told me once that the reason he doesn't go to movies anymore is because he gets embarrassed at his tears that flow at the sad ones. You could meet the real version of my friend *if* you were able to withstand the wall of protection he hides behind.

My friend epitomizes an observation I have made about we human beings: "If you've walked where I've walked and seen what I've seen then you'll know why I am." My friend wears a façade that shelters him from more of what he's experienced at an earlier time in his life. The problem with building such walls of protection is that when they get high enough, we're imprisoned and need Grace-Saturated People to help us take down the bricks.

Life Is Harsh . . . Handle with Care

Grace-Saturated People know that life can be harsh yet they treat others kindly. The saying quoted earlier, "Be nice to everyone for everyone's life is hard," is a mantra of Grace-Saturated People. Everyday life can tempt us to think that others have no reason that is acceptable for how they behave. We have to work hard at keeping clear eyes in the world we live in. Everyone is living out their lives and we often have very little, if any, understanding of what they are facing when we encounter them. This became vividly clear to me when I was in the midst of dealing with my parents' critical health conditions some years ago.

Have you ever been behind someone at a stoplight who didn't seem to notice that the light had changed to green? How did you react? Did you honk the horn (and, if so, *how* did you honk)? Stew silently? Get impatient? Something I learned first-hand during the time I was dealing with my parents' failing health is when your life is full of stresses, it's easy to miss things like the traffic light changing. Stressors such as trying to figure out if your mother is going to live and how you'll handle her death or if your father will ever recover fully from a stroke and go golfing with you again make it difficult to concentrate on other things. In short, that may have been me at that stoplight or someone like me.

Grace-Saturated People are not perfect in this area but do tend to operate in this world with a different view of how life works. They have a wisdom about people and life events that leads to giving a kinder response than many would. They don't have an ounce of "I told you so" in their blood. They do, however, have coursing through their veins the love spoken of by the apostle Peter, "Most important of all, continue to show deep love for each other, for love covers a multitude of sins" (1 Peter 4:8, NLT).

Boxes

Another characteristic of Grace-Saturated People is their passionate prophetic voice for others. In this sense I am referring to "prophetic voice" as a *calling forth* of the real person and standing against allowing a false self being placed upon others. In other words, *Grace-Saturated People celebrate the uniqueness of others and despise "boxes" for what they do to people.* Let's face it, we've all encountered "boxes" in life and felt their effect. Although I'll speak more to the issue of "boxes" in the final chapter, suffice it to say here that Grace-Saturated People see the boxes that others build for us to fit into as an assault to the unique person God has created and something to be fought off at all costs.

Grace-Saturated Relationship Building Begins in the Mirror

It may come as a surprise to others but just about every Grace-Saturated Person I know has had to come to peace with offering grace to the one they see in the mirror every morning. When I read works of authors I respect such as Henri Nouwen and Parker Palmer, I hear in their stories the struggle to live authentically. In order to live an authentic life each of us must learn to live the grace-saturated life with oneself; to offer grace to the one we walk with each day.

Let's face it, we know our raw self better than anyone else. We know all of our flaws, quirks, weaknesses, temptations, failures, and secrets. This knowledge and these memories can be like graffiti on the walls of our hearts that need the same grace we offer to others. Grace-Saturated People are that way because they must apply grace to the many layers of their lives.

Finding Grace at Home

As noted in an earlier chapter, much of what is contained in our hearts was first placed there in the earlier years of our lives. This is true also as it applies to Grace-Saturated Relationships or the lack of them. A principle that we cannot ignore is found in the Book of Proverbs: "Direct your children onto the right path, and when they are older, they will not leave it" (22:6 NLT).

There are no perfect parents so we need to give up on the idea of either having had perfect parents or ever becoming such. We need to look therefore at qualities that best provide for the children entrusted to our care. Among these qualities are the way in which we create an environment of grace for our children to grow healthy within.

Balswick, King, and Reimer in their book *The Reciprocating Self* provide some guidelines that help create such an atmosphere for positive growth. Their term for a fully functioning individual is "reciprocating self." The reciprocating self is "the self that, in all its uniqueness and fullness of being, *engages fully in relationship with another* in all its particularity." Such a person has been intentionally exposed to a relational atmosphere characterized by high levels of four essential "nutrients" for health and growth.

Unconditional Love Rather than Conditional Commitment

The first relational nutrient we need to receive is unconditional (covenant) love. This is the kind of "no strings attached" love that communicates "no matter what, you are loved." It provides a safe environment wherein we may make mistakes and not fear that we will be thrown out, severely punished, or any other negative action that invites fear into our hearts.

The lack of unconditional love is what creates an inner fear of being rejected if one would happen to miss out on the cues of others or accidentally trip over some tacit rules for relationship. Some who are reading this right now know exactly what living in a conditional world feels like. They have learned how to read early hints of rejection or judgment and found ways to respond so as not to experience the pain of rejection again.

Relationships governed by conditions tend to create an inner scrutiny whereby we never feel like we are good enough. They also invite us into the kind of lifestyle where we unconsciously approach relationships with a sense of "just tell me what you need to love me" frame of mind and heart. This also applies to our approach to God if we have been raised in relationships that are conditional. "God, just tell me what you want me to do to be pleasing to you" is the prayer many have offered up in an attempt to find a relationship with God that won't end painfully.

> *A Moment for Reflection.* Think back on your walk of faith and ask yourself if you've ever feared rejection by God. We've all heard about God's "unconditional love" but does that seem somewhat unattainable or untrue? Along with this, ask yourself how you might imagine God thinks and feels about you. Are there conditions of acceptance present? Fear of rejection? Fatigue from trying to measure up? If so, this is an area to find growth and healing.

Unconditional needs to mean just that: un-conditional. No conditions. No fine print. What is communicated verbally and non-verbally is "You are loved. Period." In our formative years we all need guidance, discipline, and, at times, punishment for behaviors so as to develop into people who know how to conduct themselves in the larger society of responsible individuals. Only when one feels unconditionally loved can such guidance, discipline, and even punishment be a form of unconditional love. In other words, in the context of unconditional love we are willing to weather our children's discontent over learning the parameters of life.

Gracing Rather than Shaming

The second relational ingredient we need is grace. I have written much on what grace looks like already but it bears repeating that showing grace to others is so important to becoming healthy. As noted above, there are a number of characteristics of Grace-Saturated People that need to be regularly displayed in parents and caregivers to the children under their care. These can be played out in a variety of everyday means.

Parents need to keep in mind what it was like when they were their children's age(s) when making comments on actions, attire, and experiences. All of us have done some things we're not proud of, so being careful not to add shame to the mix is very important when dealing with misbehavior in children. The way young people dress and groom themselves is often a reflection of trying to decide who they are and what they like to express. A brief look back at our yearbook pictures should show that fashion comes and goes but words of judgment spoken by parents seem to last a lifetime. Even how parents and caregivers respond to their children discovering their sexuality can be grounds for levels of grace or shame.

Shame is an emotion that, although similar to guilt, is different in its core message. Guilt tells us that we've done something wrong whereas shame screams there is something wrong with us. This has become evident to me in working with a number of clients over time who describe feeling unrelenting guilt only to discover that the unrelenting emotion is really shame. Guilt can be resolved by confession and making amends; shame needs grace and healing.

Empowering Rather than Controlling

A third relational ingredient that we all need is the empowerment to take control of our lives and decisions. In healthy parenting practice there is the ultimate goal of gradually giving over control of the child's life to the maturing child. This requires ongoing attention of the parent or caregiver as the child needs so much oversight early on for their protection. Electrical outlets, sharp objects, what to eat, and myriad other issues have parents making decisions for their children early on. As the child grows and matures the task of parents and caregivers is to allow the child to begin making personal decisions within guidelines. Eventually, children will be making all decisions for themselves so its so important in this hand off of power that we lessen the controls and increase empowerment to make their own decisions.

A number of parents find this to be extremely difficult to do for fear of what decisions their child will make. Fear tends to do that—making it such that their child will make the ultimate blunder (whatever that may be) if given freedom. Indeed, they may make poor decisions in their growth process but with adequate support and parameters, they will likely be able to make smaller mistakes than fear would invite us to think.

Parenting with too much control handicaps the child from discovering what they can do on their own. This approach may keep the child safe from currently making a poor decision but also deprives the child of the confidence that comes by choosing properly or learning how to recover from making bad choices. This can carry over into adult life wherein the adult child now cannot seem to make decisions with confidence.

Intimacy Rather than Isolation

The final ingredient is the provision of intimacy relationally. Intimacy is comprised of a number of actions and attitudes that convey, "You're important to me and I want you near." From the moment of birth we need the kind of closeness where we are held close and can feel the warmth of embrace.

What happens when we don't experience this kind of intimacy? We naturally begin feeling that we must not be worth loving or try to find ways to gain the attention of another. Sometimes we develop a faux intimacy whereby we can act lovingly toward others but have no inner sense of being loved. We develop a relational "hole" in our hearts that cannot be satiated outside of relationship although many other avenues can be sought out.

Isolation does not mean we literally live alone on a desert island. We can feel isolated in a room full of people. It's as if we look around and think that everyone there is connected with others and, again, what's wrong with me that it isn't that way for me? Only through a Grace-Saturated Relationship can we find the kind of healing that we need.

Building Communities of Grace

Imagine the power of being immersed in a community of people who are committed to exhibiting grace to one another. Years ago a client told me he visited a church that had the word "grace" in its name because he was so desiring to find a place like that in his life. This is the heart-cry of countless people in our world who are looking to experience grace incarnate in a community of faith. But where do we find such a place? There's the real challenge since these places don't just happen; they are intentional.

Having been a part of a church like this I can say firsthand that it was a powerful experience. I was beginning to wonder if there was such a place since my experience had been otherwise . . . even as a pastor! Was this church flawless? Nope. It had its share of flaws like any other place that houses people. Did it have a snappy building, programs, and everything else that seem to make one think of success? Nope. What did it have then? Grace and the deep love that is a part of grace. What made this church so grace-saturated? The same things that can turn any church into a grace-saturated community where people can come to find what their hearts cry out for.

Characteristics of Grace-Saturated Churches

Grace-Saturated Churches have certain characteristics in common. These characteristics create an environment wherein people can find acceptance, experience growth and healing, and offer the same to others in the larger community. Is it possible? Yes. Is it difficult to achieve? Yes. Is it worth the effort. Yes! So what do these churches have in common?

Grace-Saturated Churches have given up on formulas for success and chosen a way of being instead. I have no beef with church growth models and formulas for getting people to come to church. I simply believe that growth may have a different definition than numbers. By and large people aren't looking for a large church (numerically) to disappear into if given the opportunity to experience true depth of relationship. Interestingly, one of the "mega churches" I'm aware of really sees itself as a gathering of its small group ministries. People want to connect with others but not by simply rattling around in the same room.

Some churches seem to have a "Field of Dreams" mentality when it comes to people being drawn to their church—"if we build it, they will come." I have no qualms with buildings either but some of the excesses have left those in the community believing that churches simply want to take people's money to build and buy. God forgive us.

Grace-Saturated Churches choose to live a certain way where people and their needs are of greatest importance. These churches are full of people who have discovered, first-hand, the principle shown in the words of Jesus regarding the woman who washed his feet with her tears:

> Then turning to the woman, but speaking to Simon, he said, "Do you see this woman? I came to your home; you provided no water for my feet, but she rained tears on my feet and dried them with her hair. You gave me no greeting, but from the time I arrived she hasn't quit kissing my feet. You provided nothing for freshening up, but she has soothed my feet with perfume. Impressive, isn't it? She was forgiven many, many sins, and so she is very, very grateful. If the forgiveness is minimal, the gratitude is minimal" (Luke 7:43-47, The Message).

People who comprise Grace-Saturated Churches have become fully aware of how deeply they and others need grace.

Grace-Saturated Churches embrace the reality of the human experience. As I noted earlier, we need to give up on the notion of becoming flawless. As I've pointed out to clients over time, one of the characteristics of being human is that we make mistakes. If you're human you're going to make them. Hopefully we can learn over time enough that we lessen the number of life-altering mistakes but make mistakes we will.

In speaking with a pastor about a group I had developed for teens who have experienced the divorce of their parents, I was told in a rather straightforward manner that this church did not have any need of such a group since it didn't believe in divorce. As I hung up the phone I wondered if indeed the church did not have anyone get divorced *or* if those who, for whatever reason, became divorced no longer felt welcome to attend the church and therefore the pastor was correct. People experience divorce so the question is whether the church is a place where we accept those in pain.

When I teach counseling students about reality I draw two parallel horizontal lines on the board. I label the top line "expectations" and the bottom line "reality" and purposely place a large gap between the two and ask, "What do you think resides here?" After listening to the variety of guesses, I share with them that what resides here is "frustration"—the distance between our expectations and reality determines how frustrated we are with life "as it is" as opposed to how it "should be." Churches that have high levels of expectation of what the Christian life "looks like" when compared with the reality of experience can tacitly or openly display levels of frustration with where people find themselves.

Grace-Saturated Churches discourage hiding behaviors and foster honesty. Only churches that accept where people as they are can encourage these same people to take an honest look at how they currently live as opposed to how they could be living. A counseling maxim is that *shoulds* and *oughts* foster guilt and shame when applied to self, and *frustration* and *anger* when applied to others. When we are in an environment that understands the human condition, we feel safe to allow our guards to drop so we can take an honest look at ourselves and others.

Once we recognize our own personal "garbage can lids" that we carry to protect ourselves, and the environment that no longer needs such a defense, then we can let go of the defense and see what it feels like to have both hands free for use. To do this we must feel safe enough to be honest about our failures and foibles. Remember my friend I described earlier? If he felt as comfortable being sensitive on the outside (i.e., letting his tears fall) as he is inside, imagine the gift he would be to those around him. No prickly exterior, just the sensitive-hearted man that God created him to be.

Grace-Saturated Churches are made up of Grace-Saturated People whose view on problems is very different than that held in the general society. They see problems as just that—problems that people experience. This makes it so much easier for us to become honest about the problems that plague us.

Grace-Saturated Churches encourage the process of forgiveness. Forgiveness is one of those terms that is misunderstood. Some believe that forgiveness is synonymous to forgetting, renewed relationship, or even that what happened is okay. None of these are true and, although some relationships are renewed as a result of forgiveness, it is not the same; some relationships will never be mended. Forgiveness really needs to be viewed as a process more than an event and that forgiveness is really for the health of the person doing the forgiving.

Think for a moment about anyone you had, or have, a hard time forgiving. Remember how much that took out of you when you refrained from offering them forgiveness? It was as if they walked with you everywhere you went, attended every family gathering, and sat at every meal as an uninvited guest. Now, they weren't physically present but were fully there in your thoughts and emotions. I have told clients who were harboring unforgiveness to really get even with the person *by forgiving them.* What? Yes, the only way we can free ourselves from the inner tyranny of the one who hurt us is to learn to forgive. Failing to forgive gives the offender power over our lives whereas forgiving them sets us free from their emotional control.

Forgiveness is not an easy task. It takes continued effort and an eye toward ways in which unforgiveness can sneak back in. The process of forgiveness is akin to cleaning and tending to a wound we have. We need to cleanse and bandage the wound while protecting it from further damage so it can heal. As I teach my counseling students, forgiveness has three parts: act, process, and state. Our initial step toward forgiveness is an action that is where I *choose* to begin the process of forgiveness. Have we forgiven the person with this act? No, we have started the process. The process of forgiveness is the longest, most difficult part as it finds us making progress, experiencing set backs, and back and forth it goes until we eventually reach a state of forgiveness. We process the pain of what's been done to us, find new ways of looking at the old pain, and make some sort of meaning of the events as a part of the forgiveness journey. It's at this point that we can recall the offense but it doesn't have the pain that it used to.

But forgiveness is not just for those who have offended us. Forgiveness needs to be offered to ourselves too. Grace-Saturated Churches know that we all need to offer forgiveness, to others and self, and provide ways for people to experience this. Part of the care ministries of such churches is often a counseling component wherein people can talk freely and confidentially about what they've held against others and themselves to find healing in the process.

Grace-Saturated Churches don't give simple answers for the complex questions of life. One of the great difficulties we must overcome in this life is getting past the idea that there is an answer to, or reason for, everything. This may come as a surprise to some since we've been so enculturated to believe life is always to make sense. Grace-Saturated Churches embrace the fact that life is full of mystery and paradox. Contrary to what some might think, this approach helps deepen one's faith rather than wondering where God is in the midst of the confusion.

We can figure out many things on one level but be lost on another. For example, when we've been wounded in any of the ways I wrote about in an earlier chapter, we start to ask "Why?" fully expecting that an answer will take away the pain. But is just doesn't. So we try to make peace with the events by coming up with "reasons" that "it" happened. The thinnest level why "it" happened may be chance or being in the wrong place at the wrong time, but neither of these give any solace. So we seek to come up with a reason why. People in Grace-Saturated Churches don't offer answers when there are none; they respond by being with members who are hurting.

This is fresh in my mind after having recently come through a season of loss upon loss. Within six months time I lost to death my father, my younger sister, and then my mother. Suffice it to say, I was feeling like I could relate a bit to Job. There were no simple answers to be had nor was I seeking them. Some very Grace-Saturated People around me offered exactly what I needed: relationship. They are very intelligent people who had no answers to give but plenty of support. Grace-Saturated Churches are made up of people like these.

Grace-Saturated Churches know the immense power of relationship and seek to foster healthy ones. As noted above, people aren't looking for necessarily the snappiest, biggest church around but are looking to connect at a deeper level than is possible in many other settings. This may not be readily apparent but we all tend to have invisible "relationship antennae" that help us search out what we need when with others. Deep relationships are the key to deep health and healing. There are far too many thin and unfulfilling relationships around. But relationship building involves risk. Grace-Saturated Churches are committing to deep community over thin fellowship and are willing to take the risk.

Claude Thomas Bissell is noted as saying we should, "Care more than others think wise. Risk more than others think safe. Dream more than others think practical. Expect more than others think possible." This lies at the heart of Grace-Saturated People in their approach to others. They desire to call forth the person God has created others to be and stand against anything less. Sometimes this means standing against convention and seeing more in a person than those around them see until it dawns upon others who the person *really is.* However, this can be risky, but it comes down to what are we looking to promote, new levels of intimacy or deeper levels of isolation?

In 1 Peter 1:22 we are given an injunction to go beyond thin fellowship. "So see to it that *you really do love each other intensely with all your hearts*" (NLT, emphasis added). But what does this look like? I can say confidently that it looks much different than what a number of churches practice especially as it concerns male-female relationships.

Jesus broke all social convention by talking to the woman at the well. Men of that era did not speak to women in such a way and so he was breaking all the rules of "safety" and convention. He also had women in his entourage and in close proximity during his ministry. Mary, the woman who wiped his feet with her hair and tears, was very close to Jesus. I dare say that many in leadership today may be having a talk with Jesus about what others are saying about him in this area. But Jesus knew that men and women are needed to help in the healing and restoration process of men and women. In doing so, Jesus brought grace to relationships—do we? Or are we too afraid to risk?

When speaking at a gathering and sharing along these lines, I opened by asking, "If it were possible that God would reach down and take all the Christian men from the earth, what would it look like?" I let the question settle uncomfortably with the audience and then said, "In my experience, I don't think it would look much different than now" and continued by speaking of how, out of fear, many men wouldn't be caught dead talking alone with a woman other than their wives for fear of how it would look. Or they wouldn't consider going over to help a single mom fix something in their house alone. Fear and risk-free living.

I'm not a fan of buffet style restaurants. It's not that I don't like them, it's that I like them *too* much! I just don't trust myself with a buffet line because I skip past the greens and go right for the fried foods, meats, and, if there is room left, the dessert line. I never feel good after a buffet because I always get my money's worth. Bottom line: I don't trust me at the buffet. I don't, however, forbid others from enjoying a good buffet or lead them to believe that no one can manage such an opportunity. Too many influential leaders, writers, and speakers seem to have the same problem as me except theirs is not with the buffet, their problem is with close relationships. It would seem that their belief is that there are no healthy males but only those who, given opportunity, would surely fall to temptation if alone with a female and what assumptions does this make about the females too?

Make no mistake, I'm not naïve. I know the risks involved with relationship-building but the rewards of deep relationship so far outweigh the risks that we must risk being real with each other. In other words, we must see that our different "intimacy thresholds" can cause us to fear getting close and keep us safely isolated and insulated from those needing a close relationship that is healthy and free of exploitation.

Close relationships can go badly. Agreed. But that is more because we're not well-prepared for developing deep relationships within the Body of Christ. To paraphrase a colleague of mine, "The answer to abuse is not misuse but proper use." How do we learn to have deep relationships and is there grace when we make mistakes in this process? These are the questions that Grace-Saturated Churches are willing to take on in the pursuit of deep community.

The Greatest Commandment

Grace-Saturated Churches live out the three-fold principles of Jesus' "greatest commandment" as it pertains to building relationship. I have often wondered why it is that many followers of Christ have only paid solid attention to the first part of his answer to the Pharisees when asked about which commandment is the greatest. His answer seems to provide a balanced picture of what constitutes spiritual, psychological, and relational health and even though we can be quick to recite his words, "Love the Lord your God with all your heart, all your soul, and all your mind" and "Love your neighbor as yourself" (Matthew 22:37-39), we tend to place most of the emphasis squarely on the first part.

Is it wrong to focus on pursuing intimacy with God in an ever-increasing way? Absolutely not. It is vitally important to grow and mature in our relationship with God. We were created to enjoy fellowship with God that transcends mere knowledge of our Creator to intimacy with him. Jesus didn't stop there though and neither should we. The next two parts focus on other relationships—those with ourselves and with others.

In speaking to a group of Masters of Divinity students I posed the question, "Wouldn't it be wonderful if we followed everything Jesus commanded rather than just a portion? And wouldn't it be wonderful if in our churches we followed everything he said rather than just a part?" You might imagine that I got their attention. I then went on to encourage them to include time in their services for learning to love oneself and learning ways to let that healthy self-love flow out into active love for others. It may or may not be practical, but dedicating a third of any church service to loving God and ways of doing this, another third to finding health and healing in ourselves, and a final third of service time to developing deep community with others seems to be what Jesus was saying would fulfill all the law and prophets.

Healing Is a Journey

We are on a path to health and wholeness that is a lifelong journey. We need each other and the healing power of Grace-Saturated Relationships to make it to the destinations we are heading toward. In fact, for us to come home to our Grace-Saturated Narrative we must have Grace-Saturated Relationships to help us make it there.

7

Coming Home to Your Grace-Saturated Narrative

It was during spring break several years ago that I spent a day with my two research assistants who also were absolutely captured by the concept of narrative therapy from a Christian perspective. The more we discussed it the more we discovered something so much more rich and deep than even the tenets of narrative therapy could provide. So we set aside this day to see if we could figure out what it was.

We knew that we were discovering a pathway to living that had been overlooked and this journey took on new dimensions that spring day. As we prayed, thought out loud, and discussed where we'd been and where we were going, there came a point where the following question arose: "Is overcoming a problem-saturated narrative the end goal?" Without hesitation I heard myself say, "It's not about trying to achieve some problem-free life; it's about discovering and living our *Grace-Saturated Narrative* that's the goal." At that moment the term *Grace-Saturated Narrative* was born and came to be the focus of our research, writing, and speaking.

Grace-Saturated Narrative Defined

To come home to our Grace-Saturated Narrative (GSN) we have to first understand what it is. The term *narrative* as I use it here refers to both the *story of who we are* and the *way in which the story affects our ways of thinking, feeling, behaving, and relating.* Each of us carries around a story or narrative about ourselves. This story has been developing over our lifetime and is comprised of the many events of life and what we made of these events. It's as if we are walking books that have many chapters in them. Each of these chapters contain not only the events but, again, what these events mean to us and what they say about us and our place in the world. Some of these chapters contain resilient stories yet other chapters have stories that need healing. To attain our GSN we need to review what has been "written" on our hearts and do editing work to the story that has developed if it is keeping us from living to our fullest potential. Living out our GSN means we're living the life God designed for us which surpasses our wildest dreams.

GSN versus PSN

When our lives have been plagued by problems and adversity to the point that our narratives have become negatively affected by them, we develop a Problem-Saturated Narrative (PSN). These PSNs then dictate how we think and feel about ourselves and the ways we approach life. We wear this heavy coat of problems and get "pick-pocketed" of who God created us to be in the process. Not only does a PSN rob us of the joy God intended for us to experience in life, these narratives also define us very "thinly." An example of a "thin" definition of a person would be as noted earlier, "He's an alcoholic" instead of seeing the man as "Joe, a wonderfully gifted individual, who struggles with alcoholism. He's a loving husband, devoted father, dedicated friend, and child of God who has been discovering that problems do not define him."

Operating from a GSN perspective positions us to think, feel, behave, and relate in ways that are more in alignment for how God intended us to be. In short, when we live out our GSNs we are cooperating with God's plans to have his kingdom principles in operation on earth as they are already in place in heaven. It is only when we have a proper view of problems, understand God's rich and thick grace, and apply this to our lives do we have a chance at discovering and living out our Grace-Saturated Narrative. To risk living congruently as the people God has created us to be, we need to have such a solid footing or we will succumb to the pressure of a Problem-Saturated Narrative.

Past, Present, and Future

Discovering and living out our GSNs affects all three time frames—past, present, and future. To make peace with our *past*, we need to apply God's grace to our stories (also called "narratives") of how we and others lived back then. For some people, so much time and energy is spent living in the past without ever finding peace and freedom. It is as if they will accept life once they can fix it rather than applying God's grace to the story-telling of our past lives into the present. We do need to edit the way we tell our stories and God's grace affords us the power to do so. Without having grace for our past, we will find no grace for our present or future.

The narrative of our *present* is in process. We decide daily how we will tell the story of our lives in each moment of the day. Do I listen to the grace-less story of my past and simply continue to tell that story into my present or do I choose to narrate a grace-saturated way of approaching today? For example, if I listen to my graceless past I may see myself today as deficient in some way, think and feel poorly about myself, and act in deficiency-oriented ways toward everyday life and the relationships I have in it. My wounded past would dictating my present.

Living out of a graceless past leaves me feeling deficient not only in my past but also in the present, and I can be only marginally hopeful that my future can be any different. If, however, I listen to my GSN, I can find healing for the wounds of my past, experience the health and hope in the present to live in a different way, and see the future as a yet-to-be-experienced wonder as I become fully the person God intended me to be long before I was even a glimmer in my parents' eyes.

GSN Is More Than a Box of Chocolates

In a way, Forrest Gump was right when he said that life is like a box of chocolates wherein you just never know what you're going to get. None of us can predict what will come our way or even how we'll deal with it or find meaning in it. Like Dorothy and Toto encountered in the *Wizard of Oz*, life can change drastically in a moment and we're left trying to make sense of it all and get back to a place where we once lived. GSN involves much more than the experiencing of life and whatever it brings; it's a way of approaching life that is more active than passive.

A friend of mine was recently telling me about a cartoon he saw somewhere of two older women working in the garden together. As the one was leaving the other said, "Have a good day!" The woman turned and said, "I make days good." This woman understood that only a part of enjoying life is what happens; the more important aspect of the day is how we live it and what we do with this "box of chocolates" called life.

We develop stories about life and these stories we walk in daily contain the lenses for looking outward, inward, and upward. Outward toward life and the people we share this world with; inward toward ourselves and how we see ourselves and our place in this world; and upward in how we relate to God and the divine plan for our lives. As Griffin wisely noted, "The stories we tell ourselves, particularly the silent or barely audible ones, are very powerful." We first develop our stories and then our stories develop us. A graceless life is connected to living out a PSN whereas a grace-saturated life is tied to walking out our GSN.

There's more! Moving from living out of our PSN into a more GSN-oriented lifestyle doesn't stop with functioning in a better way. Our GSN opens our eyes to seeing ourselves as the person God has created and celebrating all of our uniqueness. You see, living out our GSN helps us go beyond mere life to the kind of life that a person lives when they are utilizing the entire person they have been created to be.

One of my richest blessings is to be able to help people identify the story they once had that no longer is being lived out fully and to encourage them to embrace who God has created them to be again, or for the very first time. One of my clients was dealing with depression and relational difficulties when we first began counseling together. In the process of meeting with him I discovered that he was an artist but had lost track of that. As he spoke of an earlier time in his life when painting was an outlet for him, I could sense he had lost that part of himself. Not only had he stopped painting, he also had lost confidence in his ability to do so. I encouraged him to reclaim this part of his life as I saw it as part of his GSN, although I didn't use that term then. He did begin painting again around the time we finished up treatment and I didn't see him again for many years.

One day while I was shopping, I met this man I had counseled years before. He was doing well but beyond the absence of the difficulties that brought him into counseling, he had pursued painting again! Not only had he decided to pick up his brushes, he told me of going through a training program that enhanced his gift and now he was painting regularly and was selling his paintings. It just so happened that where I encountered him that day was where he was working now and the employer had hung a number of his paintings in the establishment. I asked him if these were for sale and when I found out they were, I purchased one of them that simply captured me. The scene in the watercolor was appealing enough but it was his GSN shining through the painting that sealed the deal for me. I love that picture!

Too many of us get talked out of our GSNs by well-meaning, or not so well-meaning, people in our lives. The child who is discouraged when coloring because they cannot seem to "stay within the lines" can approach life from the perspective of "I'm no artist" and therefore give up on the joy that comes from expressing oneself artistically. Those around may have an interest in helping the child learn the conventions of a society that lives within the lines. Unfortunately, too much emphasis on conformity can result in the person feeling like they're living in a box.

Boxes

One of the benefits of growing up behind a shopping plaza was that we never were at a shortage of things to captivate our imaginations. Stores would throw out all kinds of things that young boys creatively turned into hours of entertainment. Among the many treasures we found were the refrigerator boxes that the Montgomery Ward store set out by the dumpsters. Unbeknownst to them and to our great delight, they threw away perfectly good castles, forts, and tunnels!

Refrigerator boxes were great fun for us even though they were never created for what we turned them into. These boxes were originally constructed for safely transporting new refrigerators from the factory to the store and eventually to the homes of those purchasing them. They were very functional but only were able to become castles when young minds turned them into such.

Unfortunately, not all boxes in life are fun or even functional. In fact, the "boxes" I encounter in my counseling practice tend to be the type that suffocates the GSN out of people. In the best scenarios, others built these kinds of "boxes" with the intention of protecting their loved ones from harm. Well-meaning people wanted to keep those under their care from getting hurt. Even though the "box" was intended to protect, often it resulted in harm. For example, some parents want to keep their children so safe that they prevent them from exploring the world in which we live. This may indeed spare their children the pain of falling down but also discourages them from taking any risks in life. Which is better, a life without bruises because of no risk or one in which the risks taken have resulted in the person's growth?

When I was in grade school, I so looked forward to gym class because I always had fun playing the different games. In looking back, however, I see that not all my classmates had the same fun as I did because of some of the "boxes" that had been built for them. A glaring example is that at that time girls were not allowed to play full court basketball. Why? To this day I don't know for sure but my best guess is that there was some belief that girls could somehow be harmed by being allowed to play beyond half court. If true, this "box" was designed to protect not harm but whatever the rationale, girls who enjoyed basketball were restrained from fully playing the sport due to the "box-building" of those in authority.

If the best-case scenario for building boxes were safety, the worst would be to control, dominate, and victimize. In my work as a pastor and counselor I've seen people even take the life-giving Word of God and use it to build boxes of control. One of those seen often is the misquoting of Scripture to have women "submit" to their husbands. Without a proper understanding of this passage of Scripture, many a woman has been subjugated to an inferior position when indeed the proper reading of such a passage says nothing of the sort!

Danger—Box-Building in Progress!

Box building has two negative aspects to it: the one is that power and control is used on others thus confining them; the other is that we internalize the boxes and sacrifice life and limb to fit into them.

When I teach a course called Narrative Approaches to Counseling, I always show a video clip of Dr. Martin Luther King Jr.'s "I Have a Dream" speech. Dr. King knew the power of societal box-building and how harmful it was when accepted as the norm. He stood against this practice to the point that it cost him his life. Those who benefitted from power and control did not stop at anything to maintain it and therefore sought to silence his voice of protest. They were unsuccessful in squelching the message of Dr. King to dismantle the confining boxes that were harming so many. Because he was willing to stand against the practice of marginalizing people because of the color of their skin, we now are making gains in this country against the devastating practice of racism.

Although racism is an extreme form of box-building, it is not the only "ism" that harms people by seeking to dismiss, disempower, and silence them. Sexism, when unchallenged, steals the voice of women and does not allow them to be fully the people God has created them to become. Ageism also relegates the young and old from contributing their gifts and perspectives with the larger population. People were never created to live in such painful boxes but, remembering John 10:10, there is a spirit at work in this world that is behind the construction of the "boxes" that steal, kill and destroy our GSNs.

This brings us to the second negative aspect of box-building. When we are indoctrinated that a particular "box" is how life is to be, we often try our best to live within the confines of these boxes. We internalize the way we are *supposed to be* to the detriment of how we were *created to be*. This, then, becomes an internalized constriction that, although it doesn't feel right, is abided by until we hear the liberating call of our GSN.

These kinds of boxes are indeed NOT what God had in mind for us. This is not only because of the pain suffered by those bruised by being stuffed into these boxes, but also because it damages our ability to attain our GSN when we to try to fit into them.

One of the ways that I choose to spend time in reflection is by utilizing what I'd call my *sanctified imagination*. In much the same way that the psalmist was able to mentally place himself in the green pastures and near the still waters of Psalm 23, I go to a mental place on the shoreline of Lake Michigan where I grew up. In my mind's eye I see myself sitting on a dune just a ways away from the shoreline overlooking the Great Lake. On one of the days when I was reflecting on my own experiences with the boxes of life, I envisioned a group of people on the beach working on a project together. I sensed in that moment the Lord coming up to me and sitting down beside me. He asked, "What are they doing?" to which I replied, "They're constructing a box." He asked, "Who's it for?" and I said, "Me." His response was an under-the-breath "Hmm" that had the tone of disagreement with what they were doing. I then said, "I think they're building one for you too." It was at this point I sensed God say, "Let's get out of here" in a way that caused me to feel he had better places and scenes for us to experience so we left together.

Mental imagery? Yes, but Spirit-infused imagery that carried with it the message of God for us to not be constrained by the world's view of how we should be when compared with God's plans for our lives. All evidence that the God who could not be contained in the box of the tomb wants his children to live in the freedom of new life as well.

Correspondence

In an earlier chapter I have spoken of *correspondence,* but there is more to be said. I first came to use the term as it relates to the various ways God speaks to us after I read it in *Reaching for the Invisible God: What Can We Expect to Find?* by Yancey. It resonated with me due to the fact that human beings tend to look for God to communicate with us in one of two ways. First, we expect God to communicate with us in much the same way as we do with others. Maybe not in hearing him speak right out loud, but somehow he would communicate clearly enough what he wants us to know especially as it pertains to important issues.

"God, just tell me what to do!" can be our heart's cry, but if we're looking for a clear, indisputable answer for many of the issues we face, we may very well become frustrated when it doesn't come. Why? Because we're looking for a clearer, more "human" answer than may be found by this approach.

Some would say that in the Bible God communicates to us all we need to know. Although this may be true regarding the principles and parameters that guide our decisions, there are many things we desire to know from God that are not so clearly discernable in the Scriptures. For example, the Bible does assure us that God will never leave us nor forsake us and also that Christ sent the Holy Spirit to be with us after his ascension so we would not be left as if orphaned. These are great promises. But how, exactly, do they play out in everyday life? This is where understanding *correspondence* helps.

The second way that we believe God should communicate with us is intuitive in nature and more in line with the concept of *correspondence.* People who desire God's communication with them do so from an approach that is better understood as an inner knowing/sensing of God speaking. You'll often hear people say things like, "God told me . . . " or "God showed me . . . " followed by some insight that was helpful, encouraging, or gave direction. Such an approach cannot be quantified or explained, it's just *known* to be from God. This is very subjective but never stands in contradiction to the principles of the written Word.

Silent Wind Chimes

A few years ago I had something happen that was one of the most heart-wrenching experiences of my life. My little dog, Molly, was very ill and had to be euthanized. I remember coming home from the veterinary office feeling sick about the illness she struggled with for months, her treatments that had failed, her final days, and saying good-bye to her after ten short years. My heart was torn wide open and feeling very raw as I let my other dog, Katy, outside that afternoon. As Katy wandered about in the backyard I stood in the doorway hurting. I so desired, so *needed,* God's comfort and just couldn't feel it. No words would help even though fellow pet owners understood and responded in such kind ways. I knew God cared but I was not in a frame of mind where sitting and reading words of comfort in Scripture would be feasible—yet I needed him near.

Then I experienced God's correspondence. It was so subtle that it could have been missed altogether but I knew what it was beyond a doubt. You see, the home we lived in was built at the highest point in town where the wind was blowing all the time. Our yard was not well developed as we had just built on a lot that had no trees or shrubs other than the ones we planted. The breeze always had my wind chimes moving, filling the air with notes from tuned pipes. That day as I stood there in the doorway, I noticed the wind chimes stood perfectly still and not one note rang out. A thought came to my mind and touched my heart, "God and all his creation is silent with me." I was not alone; I was with my heavenly Father, standing in silence together in the loss of my little companion.

Henry David Thoreau once wrote, "Let us be silent that we may hear the whisper of God." This is so true as God is speaking in many and varied ways but he does not shout for our attention. We have to develop the sensitivity to notice God speaking, hear the message, and then not succumb to talking ourselves out of the correspondence and its meaning that he sends our way. Back to the silence of the wind chimes. One could say it was a coincidence and that I was "reading into" the event. If I believed solely in a scientific approach to life, I might agree with such a statement. Science has its place, but so does the subjective experiencing of life that our faith brings. The ordering of emphases in 1 Corinthians 5:7 seems to show this to us for we are to "live by faith and not by sight" (NIV). And what is faith but "being sure of what we hope for and certain of what we do not see" (Hebrews 11:1).

Ears That Hear

There is good reason why the Scriptures encourage us to develop "ears to hear what the Spirit is saying." If we indeed are spiritual beings living in relationship with God who is spirit, then there must be spiritual sensitivities developed to communicate with him. Learning God's correspondence is necessary.

In my love of nature, I see the creativity of God everywhere from the brilliant blue flash of darting indigo buntings to the multi-hued sunsets on the Lake Michigan horizon, to the camouflage of spots on fawns in the springtime. God is an amazing artist to be sure and his artwork moves the souls of those who notice. Beyond this, he uses his creation as a means of correspondence.

One of the correspondences of God to me is the sighting of cardinals. These red birds are a favorite of mine anyway but have come to represent God's presence in my life when I need to experience it. For example, I recall a time where I just needed to know God was near and seemingly out of nowhere, a cardinal would show up. Coincidence? Maybe, but not from my perspective. You would have to be in my skin to know the absolute perfect timing with which these occurrences happen to see them as divine correspondence. That doesn't mean that every time I see a cardinal, I see it as God seeking to communicate deeply with me. However, the times when these sightings seem orchestrated to indicate that he indeed is with me are undeniable.

This is one reason why it is important to get out from our houses and offices constructed by human beings into the world that God created. This positions us to hear him speaking still. You will notice that Jesus pointed to the birds of the air and the flowers of the field to show his Father's care and how not a single bird could drop to the ground without his Father's awareness. He was sharing a lesson that was being communicated through God's creation.

In my own life I have worked to develop my ability to spiritually hear more acutely and in doing so have been so pleased at the regularity in which God desires to communicate with me. In sharing what I have found with others, I have heard reports of how difficult, at first, it was to get past the obstacle of the scientific indoctrination of our culture and the joy that came when hearing God's voice through sacred correspondences. We have to train ourselves to hear God speak and not talk ourselves out of listening in a new way because it "doesn't make sense."

Little Stories from God

Correspondences are little stories from God to us. They are timed, they are intentioned, and yet they can be missed if we overuse our reasoning abilities. Although Eugene Peterson was speaking of the stories written in Scripture, his statement holds true of the correspondences I have written about so far. "We are caught off-guard when divine revelation arrives in such ordinary garb and mistakenly think it's our job to dress it up in the latest Paris silk gown of theology, or to outfit it in a sturdy three-piece suit of ethics before we can deal with it. The simple, or not so simple, story is soon like David under Saul's armor, so encumbered with moral admonitions, theological constructs, and scholarly debates that it can hardly move" (*Eat This Book*, p. 43). We can indeed be caught off-guard with the powerful ways God communicates through his creation to the point that we may doubt their validity. Yet Jesus drew crowds of thousands to hear him share truth wrapped in the little stories of common things in life.

Meet Me Here

We come to meet with God in a variety of ways that include the classic spiritual disciplines, sanctified imagination, developing our ability to "correspond" with God, reading the words of those who are traveling this journey, and interacting with fellow journeyers.

The following in an excerpt from an e-mail message I sent to a couple friends of mine regarding the place of the spiritual disciplines in hearing God:

> One other thought for my two friends on this journey has to do with the spiritual disciplines. I believe one reason this flooded to me this morning is that today is a fasting day for me where I am opening space for God through this practice. I try to make Wednesdays a fasting day but that hasn't occurred with the regularity that I would like to have. When I do open such space it seems that clarity of thought and vision happens with regularity. I don't share this to draw attention to me, I share this to encourage both of you, my friends and fellow journeyers, to find whatever ways work best for you in opening space for God to speak his wonderful ideas to you and about you and your GSN. As I've said before, what we're working on has tremendous Kingdom potential!
>
> In short we must develop our capacity for "noticing" God speak to us in whatever way that seems best to God. Without nurturing such an ability to hear God's messages to us, we are left shy of resources in finding the healing of our souls, editing our PSNs, and discovering the GSN God has designed for us.

Abundant Life or Something Less

It has been my experience that way too many Christian folks who know they're bound for heaven really are not enjoying the trip. It's as if they have come to believe that real living only exists in the "sweet by and by" and this life is simply to be endured. How sad when we come to believe such a lie. Once such a belief is embraced, we begin living in such a way that misses the point of the passage shared earlier: "The thief comes only in order to steal and kill and destroy. *I came that they may have and enjoy life, and have it in abundance (to the full, till it overflows)*" (John 10:10, AMP, emphasis added).

Living out our GSN means we are powerfully thankful for the fact that our sins have been forgiven and we have a place awaiting us in heaven someday while also living life here on earth the way God designed it for us to live. Remember, Satan is referred to as a thief as well as a murderer so his nature is such that he desires to steal our GSN if he can. Sadly, it would appear that he is very successful in this area.

Live Until You Die

Paul Tournier once observed that some of the men he worked with had died long before their bodies gave out. Why? They were going to work every day, coming home, and doing all the right things but had lost themselves in the process. This stands in stark contrast to the GSN God has called us to live out until we die. Tournier rightly noted, "Death is the inevitable passage *to another stage of life, to be compared with birth*" (*A Listening Ear,* emphasis added). Death is not the cessation of an endurance contest but a transition from one stage of our GSN into the next stage. As noted throughout this book, life here on this planet is not what God had planned and it is a very dangerous and painful environment, but that does not change God's GSN plans for each of us. If anything, it shows us in more vivid color that living out our potential as God created in us is a way to have the light of GSN shining in some very dark places.

It has come to my attention more songs and pithy statements are springing up that point out the necessity of living right up until we make the transition Tournier wrote about. Recently on the back of a shirt I read, "Life should NOT be a journey to the grave with the intention of arriving safely in an attractive and well preserved body, but rather to skid in sideways, body thoroughly used up, totally worn out, and screaming, 'WOO HOO what a ride!'" Put in GSN terms, wouldn't it be great to have so lived out our Grace-Saturated Narrative that we are heard a mile away from the pearly gates screaming, "WOO HOO, what a ride it's been living out my GSN!" I suspect others standing in line would ask themselves, "Why didn't I live like that?"

Risk Being You

When I assist in interviewing potential interns at our counseling center I know at some point I'll say the following, "If you are selected to serve your internship here there is one thing that we ask and that is that *you* show up and *be the person God has called you to be*. Do not attempt to be someone else, someone you think we're looking for. If we select you, we want *you!*" Why do I say this? Simply because the person God has created them to be is exactly who we want here. Of course we'll help shape them in their professional counseling skills but that simply trains and refines their giftedness.

Make no mistake, living out our GSN authentically as the people God has created us to be is risky.

There is no shortage of people who would like to introduce us to the boxes that we should fit into but we must fight off "box dwelling" like the plague. Ephesians 2:10 reminds us, "For we are God's masterpiece. He has created us anew in Christ Jesus, so that we can do the good things he planned for us long ago." GSN! Risky business indeed, but so worth it!

Dare to Take the Journey

A coffee mug I purchased years ago that I use regularly admonishes me, saying, "Dare to take the journey that begins where the path ends" followed by 2 Corinthians 5:7, "For we walk by faith and not by sight." This journey of living out our GSN is one in which faith is required to step on the path each day. Why? Because people seem to prefer safety over risk and unknowingly sacrifice growth and vitality in life and settle for getting through life without much harm done.

Anyone who has ever lived their life fully and positively impacted this world as a result has done so despite the risks involved. One of the risks we encounter is that of making mistakes along the way as we forge this pathway that seemingly few travel. I don't mean we're afraid of making little mistakes of the *faux pas* variety; the type we fear are those wherein we might experience estrangement from friends and family or even the faith we currently live by.

It is entirely possible that the relationships you currently are in will be challenged to grow along with you or may need to change. As people climb out of their current boxes and live life the way God designed it to be lived, the "box builders" will likely object. I recall one such instance when I began my graduate training. I was privileged to be in a small group setting with one man who, after retiring from missions work, decided to go back to school and earn his Masters degree in counseling. In a conversation with him one day he told me how his friends weren't in favor of his plans. They had asked him, "Do you know that you'll be 62 when you finish that degree?" to which he replied, "I plan to be 62 whether I pursue the degree or not and it's something I've always wanted to do!"

People don't always agree with the pursuing of something different and among these folks are those for whom we care very much. How do we handle this? In a nutshell, we have to offer grace and patience to others who don't understand the changes that come to our lives as we respond to God's invitation to pursue our GSNs. We all need to accept the reality that people may not ever understand or agree with us. That's really nothing new since Jesus had 5,000 following him at one time yet died nearly alone.

We can fear changes to our faith as well. As a part of teaching a Crisis Counseling course, I talk about our beliefs being challenged when crisis strikes. Often people try to make sense of what has occurred by first looking at their part in it all. They might wonder what they did or didn't do that such a thing could happen. Sins and failings from the past are revisited as if possibly the reason for the current situation is God's punishment. Or the person may wonder if they had failed to do something like praying correctly for protection. Once this self-examination wears thin, the next focus is on why God didn't intervene. This puts the blame squarely on the only One in the universe who could have stopped bad things from happening and didn't. Lurking underneath both of these foci of examination is the real crux of the matter—our beliefs about how life *is supposed to work.*

We all carry with us a set of beliefs regarding how life works. Much of the contents of our belief system are what we have been taught yet some is of our own making or things we've picked up from others. False beliefs can remain intact until challenged. Using the example of a crisis, if a person believed that "Good Christians" don't experience such devastating events as happen in our world, they must now reconcile their beliefs and the reality of the situation. Some don't fare very well.

Crisis times invite us to reexamine what we believe to be true and make adjustments to deal with life as it is, not as it is supposed to be from our limited perspectives. Pursuing our GSN also involves a change in some aspects of our beliefs. This can also be risky if we choose to remain in religious groups that endorse anti-GSN beliefs. For example, some groups hold to such a thin understanding of grace that their walls of protection are so high one cannot see outside of them to catch a glimpse of the grace-saturated life.

Get Up!

Change involves a risk, which is why so many choose to remain where they are. In counseling practice I often quote a former professor of mine who said, "Until the pain of remaining the same becomes greater than the pain of change, people prefer to stay the same." Change involves risk and the pain of doing something new.

A beloved story of mine is found in John's Gospel (5:1-9). Jesus is visiting the pool of Siloam where many sick and disabled people gathered to hopefully encounter healing. In a surface reading of this story, it would seemingly appear that Jesus was being cruel to a man who couldn't walk. Nothing could be further from the truth though as Jesus' question, "Do you want to get well?" was an invitation to healing. As is the case with many of us, the man recited all the reasons he was unable to be healed. Jesus listened to him and then responded, "Get up! Pick up your mat and walk." Only as the man attempted to walk did he find the healing that brought him to the pool day after day, week after week, month after month. He took a chance on change and in the process found healing.

Come Home to Your Grace-Saturated Narrative

In much the same way as the young man in the story of the prodigal son had to return home to who he had once been, so we need to as well. As you may recall from the story, this young man who seemingly had it made became restless to the point that he abruptly gathered all that belonged to him and set out on a journey that took him far from home. We really don't know what all had happened in this young man's life that precipitated the escape we only see him entering into a world of experiences that would challenge him greatly to consider who he was and where he belonged.

One day as he was at the depths of despair it dawned on him that even being a servant at his father's home would be better than eating and living with the pigs. So he headed home, rehearsed his apology, and was surprised by the welcome his father gave him that surpassed anything he could have ever imagined! He was back home and at a place where he might come to see himself and his life in a much different light. He might actually now be better positioned to experience his GSN than had he not left in the first place.

You see, there was another young man in the prodigal son story as well—the older brother. This son stayed home, did everything "right," and resented the grace his father showed to the son who wasted his share of the inheritance. The elder son lived a safe life but one must wonder how much of his GSN he sacrificed in the process? As Jesus stated in another place, the person who has been forgiven much, loves much. Did this son understand his need for grace as well as his younger brother did now? It's very doubtful that he did.

Many reading this book feel far from home for any number of reasons. Like Dorothy and Toto, it may not have been of your own choice. You may have been caught up in deadly twisters that were not of your own making but have left you feeling alone and far from the place you know as home. For others, the choices you have made for whatever reason have landed you a long ways off the course you started on. Your need to experience the grace-saturated life that God offers is compelling yet you didn't think such a life would be possible. You can name the many ways you've failed yet feel a compelling draw to discover anew God's grace.

Others reading this book are realizing they have a GSN that has been hidden away for far too long. You really have missed a part of yourself and are poised to take it back. Something called to the depths of your soul to leave where you've been on the journey to now navigate to the place you need to be. It's high time to live out the story God created you to live no matter what the cost.

Finding Our Way Back Home

To find our way back home we need to open our hearts and minds to the new narrative, our Grace-Saturated Narrative, that God desires to show us.

It is not something that happens overnight or in a vacuum, it is a process of change that involves perseverance and patience.

Someone once said that "Writing is re-writing" and this is definitely true of our lives. We need to edit our distortions and begin gaining an idea of who we were created to be, offering the grace necessary for growth to ourselves and others, risking to live fully "out of the box" created by others, and finding others on this same journey who can encourage us to grow as we do the same for them. And never forget, this is a journey with God and God will help us discover our GSNs. Donald Miller, author of *A Million Miles in a Thousand Years,* wrote, "I believe there is a writer outside ourselves, plotting a better story for us, interacting with us, even, and whispering a better story into our consciousness." Jesus as the "Author" (originator) and "Finisher" of our faith, of which our narrative/story is a part (Hebrews 12:2) has such a desire to see his children live out the lives he has designed for them—a *much better story* than anyone else could have conceived.

Our Research Was Researching Us!

On that spring day that I met with my research assistants we thought we were meeting to pull together our respective contributions to the work. We soon found that this was much more than research—we discovered that what we were researching was alive and was actually researching us!

Let me explain. As followers of Christ who are professional counselors, we are all about helping people not only find healing in their lives but also discover the rich and full lives they were created for—the abundant life spoken of in John 10:10. As all counselors know, the person of the counselor is the most effective "tool" in helping our clients. Counselors don't need to be flawless or have it all together but they do need to be willing to "practice what we preach" and attend to "our stuff" as we're seeking to help others with theirs. So in our personal journeys of discovering who we are in him, we have also been pleasantly surprised at the many things we've found that seemed to be waiting for us.

Helping others find and live their Grace-Saturated Narratives began at home so to speak. The three of us had to apply what we were finding in our research to our own lives before we could ever "go live" with it. I wish I had a nickel for every time we said to one another, "Our research seems to be researching us" as we sensed a real drawing of the Spirit to keep walking the pathway we were on.

All three of us found that we had to revisit places in our own lives to see what "boxes" had constrained us and how we broke free of them to be the people God intended us to be. We had to review the stories/narratives we were living out to see if, indeed, they needed adjustment so as to empower us to live daily in a way that promoted growth and fought stagnation. We had to ask ourselves how much were we willing to risk to live authentically without apology. And we grew in new dimensions of "hearing" God speak in our lives.

The following e-mail message shared with my two research assistants gives evidence of how God was working:

> In my devotional reading this morning I was in John 14 and the most unbelievable thing happened—GSN was waiting for me! It was as if I waded into the Sea of Grace and as I was standing knee deep in it, the waves began rolling in, verse after verse, until my notebook had 2 pages of scribbling. I just had to share a few of these with you especially in light of yesterday's conversation.
>
> Here goes. Starting with verse 1, Jesus says, "Don't be troubled. You trust God, now trust me." The words "trust me" washed over me as I thought of the process of God helping us through our "stuff" to discover his GSN of our lives so it came as an underlying foundational statement.
>
> Then I read verse 6 and the waves of grace gained strength, "I am the way, the truth, and the life. No one can come to the Father except through me." Wow, he laid it out for the GSN approach—he is the Way (not the "answer"; he is the way, the path, the avenue of grace); he is the Truth (as opposed to distortions, lies, etc.) which tells me he knows the true me/you/others, not the false me/you/others (i.e., he knows *my* name, *my* GSN, the name on *my* white stone); and He is the Life (John 10:10 and all of the Gospel of John).
>
> If that wasn't enough, another huge wave rolled in that is connected with verse 8 and the God concept—"Lord, show us the Father and we will be satisfied." To which Jesus responded, "Anyone who has seen me has seen the Father!" (v. 9). The wave of grace that rolled in on me was that the Author and Finisher of our GSN (Jesus) reflects the Father's heart and is the only way of discovering and editing our GSN. I was getting "soaked" by grace at this point but it didn't stop there (talk about so many thoughts that one can't contain them? Like trying to turn our back toward the sea so that the waves don't knock us down; they just splash us around like kids in the surf!)

Verses 15 and following speak to the Spirit being sent and (brace yourself) verse 17 reads, "He is the Holy Spirit, who *leads into all truth*. The world at large cannot receive him, because it *isn't looking for him* and *doesn't recognize him*. But *you do . . .*" Wow! This connects so much with "correspondence" and becoming spiritually sensitized to hearing/seeing the Spirit in our lives. I know the original text is speaking of those who don't know Christ *but*, I think it has application to followers of his who haven't quite "learned the Shepherd's voice" and therefore are prone to "follow the thief's voice more easily." That was a *huge* wave that rolled in since we just talked of that yesterday and got "thickened" this morning!

More waves rolled in after that big one such as verse 20, " . . .I am in my Father, and you are in me, and I am in you." Talk about our security being affirmed in our GSN work! Then, in verse 21, "I will reveal myself to each one of them . . ." Truly his followers are being pursued! He desires to reveal himself and our GSN to us and finds creative ways of doing so.

Then, as the waves of grace started to recede, verse 26 solidly said, "He (the Holy Spirit) will teach you everything and remind you of everything I have told you." The Holy Spirit as empowerer, teacher, and the one who helps "thicken" our GSN!

Closing Thoughts

As we part ways, my prayer for you is that you continue on this journey of hope and healing. Never forget that you are not alone but that there are many sojourners on this path as well. Seek out these Grace-Saturated Relationships and strive to be one to someone else. We need each other and the encouragement that comes when together to keep walking. We're not "home" yet and need to understand so much about the journey. It is my hope that the words I've shared have been helpful to you and that they encourage you to keep walking in the direction of God's Grace-Saturated Narrative for you.

Bibliography

Balswick, Jack O., et al. *The Reciprocating Self: Human Development in Theological Perspective.* Downers Grove, IL: InterVarsity, 2005.

Barclay, W. *The Gospel of Matthew.* Louisville, KY: Westminster John Knox Press, 2001.

Jones, M.J. *The Color of God: The Concept of God in Afro-American Thought.* Macon, GA: Mercer University, 1987.

McMinn, M.R. *Sin and Grace in Christian Counseling: An Integrative Paradigm.* Downers Grove, IL: IVP Academic, 2008.

Miller, D. *A Million Miles in a Thousand Years; What I Learned While Editing My Life.* Nashville: Thomas Nelson, 2009.

Nichols, M.P., and Richard C. Schwartz. *Family Therapy: Concepts and Methods.* Boston: Allyn & Bacon, 2006.

Nouwen, H.J.M. *The Living Reminder: Service and Prayer in Memory of Jesus Christ.* New York: Seabury Press, 1981.

Palmer, P.J. *The Courage to Teach.* San Francisco: Jossey-Bass, 1998.

Peck, M.S. *The Road Less Traveled: A New Psychology of Love, Traditional Values and Spiritual Growth.* New York: Simon & Schuster, 1978.

Peterson, E.H. *Eat This Book.* Grand Rapids: William B. Eerdmans, 2006.

Phillips, J.B. *Your God is Too Small.* New York: The Macmillan Company, 1960.

Tournier, P. *A Listening Ear: Reflections on Christian Caring.* Minneapolis: Augsburg, 1984.

Worthington, E. L. *Hope-Focused Marriage Counseling: A Guide to Brief Therapy.* Downers Grove, IL: InterVarsity, 2005.

Yancey, P. *Reaching for the Invisible God: What Can We Expect to Find?* Grand Rapids: Zondervan, 2000.

Young, W.P. *The Shack.* Los Angeles: Windblown Media, 2007.

Made in United States
North Haven, CT
17 April 2022

18353487R00072